COURAGE

P.36

COURAGE
JON JOHNSTON

VICTOR BOOKS®

A DIVISION OF SCRIPTURE PRESS PUBLICATIONS INC.
USA CANADA ENGLAND

Unless otherwise indicated, Scripture quotations are from the *Holy Bible, New International Version,* © 1973, 1978, 1984, International Bible Society. Used by permission of Zondervan Bible Publishers. Quotations marked RSV are taken from the *Revised Standard Version of the Bible,* © 1946, 1952, 1971, 1973. Quotations marked TLB are taken from *The Living Bible,* © 1971, Tyndale House Publishers, Wheaton, IL 60189. Used by permission. Quotations marked KJV are taken from the *Authorized (King James) Version.*

The poem, "Myself," by Edgar A. Guest on p. 90 reprinted from *The Collected Verse of Edgar A. Guest* © 1934 by Contemporary Books, Inc.

Library of Congress Cataloging-in-Publication Data

Johnston, Jon.
  Courage / Jon Johnston.
    p. cm.
  Includes bibliographical references.
  ISBN 0-89693-794-1
  1. Courage—Religious aspects—Christianity.   I. Title.
BV4647.C75C64 1990
241'.4—dc20   89-49765
                                             CIP

---

2 3 4 5 6 7 8 9 10 Printing/Year 94 93 92 91 90

CONTENTS

Dedicated to
the devoted
brothers and sisters
of our
neighborhood Bible study

whose lives,
prayers,
and encouragement have
provided me with
continual
courage transfusions

FOREWORD

Several years ago, I had the privilege of spending time with Mother Teresa in Calcutta, India. As we walked through the city's streets, I found myself overwhelmed by the poverty and suffering surrounding us. Finally, I asked Mother Teresa if she did not grow discouraged facing the enormity of need in Calcutta and in the thousands of other places like it around the world. She responded: "God does not ask me to be successful. He only asked me to be faithful."

There are a thousand and one reasons why Mother Teresa should give up her work, give in to the suffering. But there is one reason why she should continue: to be faithful to her calling. Her example provides a marvelous context for this book.

What is this thing we call courage? And what does it mean in the lives of those of us who have accepted Christ? Mother Teresa's words define it as remaining faithful to one's calling despite the odds. In the following pages Dr. Jon Johnston expands on this theme and attempts to define this word in the context of a secular world which does not seem to reward real courage, in a secular world full of a thousand and one reasons not to act.

The courage about which he writes, the courage which comes from faithfulness, is a tall order indeed. The courage of faithfulness requires that we struggle against the tide, that we take unpopular stands, that we reach out to those in need. Ultimately it requires that we ignore those thousand and one reasons not to act and follow the witness of Christ.

Jesus Christ lived in a world much like ours today, a society which looked dimly upon those who walked with the poor, who reached out to the sick or spoke uncomfortable truths. But He persevered, faithful to His Father's will, a man of courage. With the same needs continuing to confront us today as faced

7

Christ on earth, the challenge to be courageous remains. Of course, it is far easier to mouth words than it is to live faithfully. Christians are also avowed sinners who acknowledge succumbing to the temptation to avert their eyes and join the crowd. In Christ we find not only the example of courage, but the power to be forgiven for our failures. Each day offers anew the opportunity to begin again a life of faithfulness—to demonstrate courage.

Senator Mark Hatfield

INTRODUCTION

I've thought long and hard about the wisdom of writing a book on courage. My conclusion: There are many reasons *not* to do it.

For one thing, books pertaining to this virtue are about as rare as sand on Southern California beaches.

Also, those who dislike me might use my words to incriminate *me*—pointing out my numerous foibles and shortcomings. Wasn't it Shakespeare who declared, "Oh that my enemy would write a book"?

But then I ran head-on into some unanticipated situations that called for taking a stand. At first it was exhilarating to follow the urgings of my conscience in the direction of right. Yet I soon experienced some backlash reactions which surprised and distressed me.

Questions began to surface. I asked myself if being courageous, even for noble causes, was really worth the hassle. Wouldn't it have made more sense to have sidestepped issues? To have gone along with the crowd? To have taken the easy way and let nature take her course? Did I really need to create this self-imposed grief?

All of this prompted me to do some intense soul-searching on the subject of courage—in my own life and in the lives of others.

I had always maintained that cowardice is a killer. It smothers joy, kills hope, annihilates love—and causes the relinquishment of the most noble qualities of character—by default.

By contrast, I'd always believed courage to have the opposite effect. It provides fulfillment, gives purpose, and invigorates the soul. And it would seem that most agree. That's why nations give medals to, and name streets after, the courageous—while cowards are despised, mocked, and often reduced to shame and remorse.

So why, when faced with some high-pressure situations, was I tempted to second-guess those actions which required a little moral mettle on my part?

To answer these questions I began to study people around me, and soon I observed many who *were* courageous in quiet, unassuming, unheralded, yet costly ways. This was heartwarming to discover.

At the same time I also noticed what seemed to be a rising tide of cowardice: more and more people refusing to take unpopular, uncompromising stands on crucial issues—especially those that are guaranteed to cause personal discomfort.

The results of increased cowardice can be seen everywhere. People in distress are ignored. Business shenanigans proliferate unchecked. Dangerous criminals are not testified against.

Not only did I see people avoiding the call to courage, I also observed scores of people acting in a truly courageous manner but in ways that were insignificant, petty, and self-serving. They were busy taking bold stands against trivial issues—creating a "tempest in a teapot"! Theirs' was a kind of courageous non-courage.

How about the church? Well, I discovered that few of us who claim to be Christ's servants really tackle the causes that are closest to His heart: Defending the weak. Fighting for justice. Countering compromise and deception within the church.

Just as in the secular society, many of us in the church shy away completely from taking strong stands. Then there are those of us who get caught up in championing causes of little consequence. In so doing, we give ourselves the illusion that we are being heroic. Theologians argue fine points of doctrine, for instance, while leaving cardinal, biblical principles unclarified. Ecclesiastical bureaucrats constantly jockey for position on their political ladders, while seeking to offend no one and gloss over essential inconsistencies. Pastors increasingly adopt the philosophy of the cancer cell: growth and growth alone—in numbers, dollars, and buildings.

Finally, instead of seeking ways and means of more closely

living out the Master's example, most laymen seem intent on getting by. Their most frequent unasked question is: "What can I get away with and still be considered a Christian?"

All of these impressions have driven me to books, to soul-searching, and to my knees. If courage is ebbing away from our nation, and particularly from God's church, something must be done without delay.

This book claims to do little more than "put a finger in the dike," and call for help. It is hoped that the readers will pick up the torch and dauntlessly march forward into battle.

To begin with, we must become sensitized to the special need for courage in our day. There is no substitute. And without courage we can have no relief.

With these heartfelt thoughts I hereby contribute "one more grain of sand."

Jon Johnston
Malibu, California

SECTION ONE

COURAGE:
What Is It?

CHAPTER ONE

Rough and Tough—or All Bluff?

"Mountain climbers connect themselves to one another with a rope to keep the one at the end from going home." (Charles Swindoll)

"He has not learned the lesson of life who does not every day surmount a fear." (Ralph Waldo Emerson)

"God does not give us an overcoming life; He gives us life as we overcome." (Oswald Chambers)

Sam, don't you ever ever say that word in this house!"

Doro LeBlond, daughter of George Bush, fired this volley of rebuking words at her son when he used the word "wimp." Why? Because the press had relentlessly accused his grandfather of being one.[1]

Her mother, Barbara, showed equal abhorrence of the descriptor in a magazine article entitled "Don't Call My Husband a Wimp."

Like the Bushes, other world leaders are deeply repulsed by any insinuation of being wimpish. And they have gone to great lengths to cast off the stigma.

Mexico's President, Carlos Salinas, has aggressively tackled corruption, drugs, and his country's foreign debt. The result? In contrast to his early days in office, he is no longer seen as a

---

1. M.G. Warner, "Bush Battles the Wimp Factor," *Newsweek*, October 19, 1987, pp. 28-31.

political weakling. *Time* magazine tells his story in an article called "Wimp No More."[2]

Prince Charles—labeled "the wimpish clown prince" by British tabloids, has been somewhat of an embarrassment to the royal family. His father, Phillip, has continually bullied Charles to "toughen him up"—calling him a "wet" (British for wimp) and taking sadistic measures that border on cruelty.[3]

Prince Charles has responded with a vengeance. He now plays a very spirited game of polo, flies aircraft at hair-raising velocities, and champions ambitious nationwide campaigns that benefit the poor and the environment. Exit Mr. Wimp. Now the press must content itself with restricting criticism to his trend-setting wife and rambunctious children.

Perhaps you are asking yourself, "What's so offensive about being called a wimp?" Let's begin by investigating its meaning. One dictionary says it's a slang term that means "a weak and ineffectual person." But its earliest known meaning extends back to 1909 at Cambridge University. Then it meant "a young, immature undergraduate girl."[4]

Some conjecture that "wimp" is a word that attempts to combine "wet" and "limp," in order to describe a person whose backbone is like spaghetti. Others say that it is somehow connected with the word, "whimper," which is something a crybaby does.[5]

For any world leader, creating an image of boldness is an absolute necessity. We might understand a leader's resentment when called a wimp. But how about the rest of us? Are we, likewise, offended by anyone who tags us with this stigma?

2. Guy D. Garcia, "Wimp No More," *Time*, April 24, 1989, pp. 28-29.
3. Brad Darrach, "Prince Charles: A Dangerous Age," *People*, October 31, 1988, pp. 97-101.
4. *New World Dictionary* (Cleveland, Ohio: William Colliers Publishers, Inc., 1980), p. 1628.
5. The first indication of the term's use in the United States occurred in 1920. It was applied to a character in a book, entitled, *Handmade Fables:* "The next day he sought out the dejected *wimp*."
Oxford English Dictionary, 1989 edition (Oxford: The University Press).

Gentlemen, Take a Bow

You bet. On one hand, we laugh at wimpishness in leaders and even in our animals.[6] I'm reminded of my mother-in-law's dog, who nearly had a nervous breakdown when a tiny mouse ran across the floor. Can you imagine what his reaction might have been at the sight of a real burglar? Coco was a canine wimp.

But it's no laughing matter when *we* are the ones being accused of possessing this disreputable characteristic—especially if we are males.

In fact the term "wimp" is almost exclusively directed at us men. And this starts early in our lives.

Boys are allowed to be "marshmallows" but usually only up to a point. Unlike what parents expect from our sisters, they expect us to defend ourselves against playground bullies, do rigorous chores around the house, and perform like champions on soccer and football fields.

Granted, our female counterparts are more involved in sports than in times past, but there still exists a gender gap. In subtle ways, the ones made of "sugar and spice and everything nice" are cautioned about appearing excessively "tomboyish."

As children grow into the high school years, the same rigid expectations are apparent, though revealed in different ways.

Popular speaker and author, Anthony Campolo, delights in describing the "jocks" (athletes) at his inner-city high school in Philadelphia.

They were so "bad," says Tony, that it was necessary to have an obituary column in the school paper! These guys didn't

---

6. *Circus elephants* can be considered little more than two-ton wimps! As adults, all that's necessary to keep them stationary is a thin rope staked to the ground. They recall tugging and pulling against such a rope to escape, when very young. At some point back then, they completely gave up—not temporarily but for life. Grown to gigantic proportions, it would be a small task to uproot the stake and be on their way. But their minds are "heavily chained."

Need another example of wimpish animals? L.M. Boyd, in the *Los Angeles Examiner* (June 24, 1989, p. 2) entitles his column "Ostriches Find Thorns a Pain in the Face." In it, he explains that (in addition to burying their heads in the sand when danger is thought to be approaching), ostriches are spooked by the sight of anything thorny. They are "face shy"—fearful of a poke in the eye. Safari goers can drive alongside them, at 50-mph, and wave a thorntree branch in their faces, and they will immediately "slam on the brakes."

walk down the halls like ordinary students, instead, they "moved." Their medal-laden lettermen sweaters were so long that they dragged along the floor. The girls were so impressed with these guys that they stood to one side and sang "How Great Thou Art."

But there were also the wimps—whom everyone treated like pariahs. Talk about being conspicuous. It was impossible to *not* recognize them. They were the ones who wore galoshes (with pants tucked inside them) when it rained or carried their lunch in a brown paper bag—and *saved the bag*.

Dr. Campolo's high school was probably not all that different from the ones we attended. At my alma mater in Bell, California, there were the same well-defined camps of males: machos and wimps.

The former were popular, fulfilled, and in sync with the girls' dreams. The latter were ostracized by all—including themselves. They invariably ended up being consumed by nagging self-doubts, antisocial activities, and intense loneliness. Their options seemed restricted to joining the chess club, becoming a library hermit, or hanging out at the local bowling alley.

So much for childhood and adolescence. Of course, males grow out of such a mentality as they enter adulthood. Right? Wrong.

Third Verse, Same as the First

Certainly females are never completely exempt from criticism for being excessively wimpish. Avoiding challenges, being given to excessive pampering or cattiness, and always feigning helplessness invites some rebuke, especially from assertive members of their own sex.

But again, we males who exhibit such behavior are more severely stigmatized. That's why we often react so vehemently at the slightest hint of accusation. Furthermore, many of us overcompensate in the opposite direction—becoming real "he-men"—to prove accusers wrong.

Question: What perpetuates this kind of thinking among us? Here are a few possible influences to consider:

1. *Macho media models are lauded in our culture.* From John Wayne to Clint Eastwood to Sylvester Stallone, the message comes out loud and clear: maleness and machismo are intertwined, or should be.

2. *Athletes capture our fondest admiration.* In perpetuating a "smash your opponent" image, jocks appear to be invincible. This is why baseball players sound gruff, and never rub a bruise caused by a 98-mph fastball.

3. *Novelists have perpetuated an idealized image of the hardy, western cowboy,* who Charles Swindoll describes as: "(The) self-sufficient frontiersman—the squint-eyed, close-lipped, saddle-hardened, rawboned fella who needs no one, trusts no one, and leans on no one (except maybe his horse)."[7]

4. *Some have (wrongly I feel), interpreted the Bible to advocate a super-man model.* In this model authoritative men make women kowtow and children cringe. Intimidation is the order of the day. The child is not "spared," nor, for that matter, is anyone else.

Such influences have pushed some of us into the arena of excess. As a result, some have become rather crude and insensitive—a cross between a bulldozer and a pit bull.

Then there are others of us who reject machomania, but who are likewise very uncomfortable with the opposite extreme: unisex. We feel that, while men and women must be equally respected, they need not be alike. At this point, allow me to call an official time-out and reveal a wrinkle or two in my own psyche. Though it's no big deal with me, permit me to explain why I tend to see myself in this camp.

Time to Own Up

Now, please don't think me prepared to join a motorcycle gang, free-fall over the Grand Canyon, or rip off bandages, if I

---

7. Charles R. Swindoll, *Growing Deep in the Christian Life: Returning to Our Roots* (Minneapolis, Minn.: Billy Graham Evangelistic Association, 1986), p. 349.

confess to not wanting to be considered wimpishly effeminate.

Given that admission, you might expect that I would shy away from certain behaviors that I (or others) might associate with that image. To be candid, some things I see men doing today seem about as manly as hosting a baby shower or shopping for doilies.

Here are some wimpish activities I find personally unappealing:

- *Wearing a diamond earring*—even if the person is a 300-pound tackle for the Chicago Bears.
- *Playing with a sponge football.* (It may be the current rage, but seems about as masculine as intercepting a powder puff.)
- *Having name monograms embroidered on shirtsleeve cuffs.*
- *Doing needlepoint.* (Go ahead, Rosie Greer, do it if you want to. I won't try to stop you.)
- *Embracing pink as a favorite color.*[8] (What brave nation ever went to battle waving a pink flag?)
- *Sporting fake-macho attire.* (Clothes designer, Danya Padilla, offers the "sweat T-shirt" for those who hate exercise, but want to look like a post-workout Marcus Allen. It is faded grey, with imprinted sweat marks.)

OK. So my preferences may seem a bit traditional as I attempt to keep some distance between myself and wimpish characteristics. But why do I have this mild case of wimpphobia? And why do so many of us guys—from world leaders to teenagers—share similar sentiments?

---

8. The color pink, evidently, has an emasculating effect. Traditionally, it has been reserved for such mild-mannered uses as little girls' rooms, bath soap, baby clothes, and bubble gum. But that is changing as a result of scientific color studies. It was found that the specific shade of Baker-Miller pink actually curbs aggression and saps energy. (Of the 153 subjects tested by Tacoma, Washington's Institute for Biosocial Research, all but two succumbed to the mood-inducing color which affects the body's endocrine system and hormones, thereby slowing the heart.)

Some prisons (e.g., San Jose, Calif.) with pink walls have been able to reduce the number of guards.

"Think Pink," *Campus Life*, January 1981, p. 30.

With a Capital "C"

Wimpishness connotes such things as being sissified, spine-less, comfort-obsessed, passive, and overprotective. But, more than anything else, it seems to imply *lacking courage.*

Among all the nations of the world, courage counts big—with but a few scattered exceptions.[9] Furthermore, courage has assumed center stage throughout history. The ancient Egyptians gloried in their bravery, as did the Assyrians, Baby-lonians, Persians, Romans,[10] and Greeks.

In our twentieth century, we stand in awe when someone mentions Japanese kamikaze pilots,[11] Afghan rebels, or China's heroic students.[12]

Courage is a virtue not confined to any race, generation, or religion. It is ubiquitous and admired by all—even in one's enemies.

---

9. Anthropologist G. Gorer lists societies whose primary goal is peaceful iso-lation rather than conquest. These include the Arapesh of New Guinea, the Lepchas of Sikkim in the Himalayas, and the Pygmies of the Congo.

The social scientist notes that these societies have these three things in common:
- Reside in inaccessible places, which other groups do not covet nor attempt to take from them,
- Orient themselves, primarily, toward the simple, concrete pleasures of life—eating, drinking, sex—and when these are satisfied, so are they,
- Make few distinctions between males and females (e.g., no attempt is made to project an image of brave, aggressive masculinity).

Lawrence S. Wrightsman, *Social Psychology in the Seventies* (Belmont, Calif.: Brooks/Cole Publishing Company, 1972), pp. 173-4.

10. The ancient Romans purposely designed their soldiers' uniforms so that the backs were exposed and unprotected. Why? It would deter them from ever considering retreat a viable option.

11. During the summer of 1944 the Japanese navy had developed a devastating rocket-propelled missile to launch from their huge attack bomber planes. But they lacked a reliable guidance system. The decision was made: Men would be put inside the bombs. Human guidance systems would steer the missiles.

The kamikaze aircraft was designed strictly for one-way, suicide missions. Named Ohka, or exploding cherry blossom, its wings and tail were made of wood.

The 15 Ohka pilots who flew that first mission sent fingernail clips and tufts of hair so their parents could hold funeral services at Yasukuni Shrine. The brave warriors penned their own eulogies such as, "I shall fall, smiling and singing songs."

Kamikaze planes were disastrous for Japan. Commanders underestimated the targeted U.S. Naval fleet. Altogether 160 "Thunder Gods" were killed, in-cluding the 15 Ohka pilots.

Author Charles Edward Jefferson states: "Three words . . . pierce the heart to the very center: one is thief, the second is liar, the third is coward. [And] coward is the most damning of them all."[13]

If this is so, no word excites and motivates the human spirit more than "courage." Furthermore, no virtue is more needed today.

Samuel Johnson, renowned eighteenth-century English lexicographer, writer, and critic, put it succinctly: "Where courage is not, no other virtue can survive except by accident."[14]

The term, "courage" is an integral part of our vocabulary. On a daily basis, we seek en*courage*ment, what someone has aptly called "courage transfusion." Ideas or people who help us face the world with boldness are greatly treasured. Conversely, we seek escape from dis*courage*ment. Negativism and "downers" seem to suck all the oxygen from the air we breathe. They throw cold water on the coals of hope.[15]

Unlike machismo, courage is a sterling quality of character that both men and women can equally aspire to. There is little that separates Joan of Arc and David Livingston—when it comes to manifesting this great virtue. It is as admirable in one sex as in another.

Likewise, authentic courage bursts the boundaries of age.

Clark Brooks, "The Ultimate Loyalty? Remembering Japan's Kamikaze Pilots," *Los Angeles Examiner,* May 29, 1989, pp. B1-B2.

12. The author visited the People's Republic of China just prior to the June 3, 1989 massacre—accompanied by Pepperdine University students. As our students intermingled with, and intensely interviewed, Beijing students, it was apparent that the latter manifested exemplary idealism and courage. No sacrifice seemed too great. Every barrier would be removed. Though now repressed, these students and their freedom-loving countrymen still share this dream.

13. Charles Edward Jefferson, *The Character of Jesus* (New York: Grosset and Dunlap, 1908), pp. 283-284.

14. Quoted by C.S. Lewis in his classic work, *Surprised by Joy* (New York: Harcourt, Brace and World, Inc., 1955), p. 161.

15. According to studies described by minister Earl Lee, five courageous, positive persons are required to merely cancel out the gloomy atmosphere created by one cowardly, negative individual. Implication: Most organizations cannot afford the luxury of having an inordinate number of cowardly, negative members.

Never shall I forget a recent interview featuring a young child with cancer, painfully but gallantly facing his imminent death.

Courage transcends time as well as space. It is no one nation's sole possession, nor does it belong to any particular age. Furthermore, it is a virtue that is expandable to permeate vast civilizations, and retractable to isolated individuals. And whenever, wherever, and however it appears, people are made to stand tall.

Nevertheless, courage is far more complex than what meets the eye—as is frequently so with life's greatest virtues. We must, therefore, venture far beyond the glib definitions and platitudes that the naive and less informed have disclosed. We must actively plumb the depths of its rich meanings, with open minds and hearts. Then we will see for ourselves why it is so esteemed by all peoples.

And we'll see why courage is absolutely essential for those of us who choose to follow the most courageous Man this world has ever known.

CHAPTER TWO

A Tree, a Horse, and Plenty of Distance

"Old age isn't for cowards." (Bette Davis)

*"A coward dies a thousand deaths; the valiant dies but once."
(Julius Caesar)*

"The worst human disaster can be met with courage and gallantry when we meet it with God." (William Barclay)

Most of us have had to endure people who constantly brag about some famous ancestor. We're told that this person had unparalleled courage and, as a result, was always triumphant in spite of unbelievable odds.

This bigger-than-life stalwart is reputed to have come on the nightmarish voyage of the Mayflower, single-handedly tamed the western frontier, or annihilated some menacing "Goliath."

Unfortunately, the Johnston lineage lacks such a folkloric hero, by a long shot. No popes, martyrs, nobles, reformers, or celebrities are in our history. I've caught myself wishing that I were, at least, related to the owner of Johnston's Pie Company!

But before I evoke excessive sympathy, allow me to drop one family name. Help me decide whether this man qualifies as a famous ancestor. I recall his name always popping up at family reunions.

Joseph E. Johnston. Ever heard of him? To say no is to betray ignorance of Civil War history.

General Joe commanded a sizable portion of the Confederate Army. His battle record earned him Robert E. Lee's highest respect. So when it came time to repel the North's ruthless General Sherman, at Atlanta, Johnston was moved from Chattanooga to take command.

Well, that's about all I knew about the courageous battle fox until we visited Atlanta some time ago. We seized the opportunity to see "Cyclo-rama," a huge, circular painting of that famous battle. In this amazing work of art, the armies and terrain are vividly shown in three dimensions. And the account of the bloody battle is audibly presented.[1]

Trying not to be too conspicuous, I squinted to see my famous relative. Finally, the recorded voice pointed him out.

Are you ready for this? During the heat of the battle, old "blood-and-guts Joseph" was depicted as sitting leisurely on his horse under a shaded tree. Oh yes, one more thing. The tree, horse, and Joseph were on the peak of a mountain that overlooked the city.

You might say that he established a generous "safety zone" between himself and the battle.

From the start, he had opposed fighting the battle—thinking that the killing, burning, and carnage would serve no useful purpose. And, he had recommended a strategy of *"retreating to establish better position."*

When this was reported to Stonewall Jackson, he was so angry that he saw to it that Johnston was relieved of his post. General John Bell Hood assumed command.[2]

So much for ancestral bravery! When the real battle ap-

---

1. The painting of the battle was done by 11 German, Austrian, and Polish painters. They spent one year in Atlanta, doing research and drawing sketches. Then they went to the American Panorama Studio, owned by William Wehner, in Milwaukee, Wisconsin, to complete the actual painting. It is round (cyclorama), but also has a three-dimensional foreground (diorama)—so that figures seem to be emerging from the painting.

2. The Battle of Atlanta was fought on July 22, 1864. There were a total of 11,722 killed. Of these, 3,722 were from the Union Army (12 percent of their soldiers) and 8,000 were from the Confederate Army (22 percent of their fighting force). The Union Army won and, as was customary with cities that resisted General Sherman's "march to the sea," Atlanta succumbed to flames and pillage.

Mark M. Boatner III, *Civil War Dictionary* (New York: David McCay, 1959), pp. 28-30.

proached, Joseph E. wasn't around. His military cronies must have thought him to be little more than "soggy milk toast." Or, in a phrase author Charles Swindoll likes to use, my forefather was perceived as a "yellow-livered mountain of jello."

But that's him—and back then. What about us today? Do we frequently showcase unmistakable doses of raw courage?

It's All in a Day's Existence

According to some, those of us who get married, eat processed food, breathe polluted air, and even get up in the morning exhibit significant courage.

Situations that demand bold responses constantly present themselves. Do any of these sound familiar?

Courage is:

- retrieving your wayward golf shot that has just shattered the window of an approaching car;
- changing careers at 55, after being fired because your company tried to escape paying retirement;
- proposing marriage to someone who has turned down three proposals in the last month;
- sliding headfirst into home plate;
- staying calm after the captain has just announced that the number two engine is on fire;
- telling your spouse that you know he or she is having an affair;
- going for counseling, even though you feel you're not at fault;
- opening the envelope that contains your undisciplined child's report card;
- agreeing to live with your mother-in-law;
- going for a mammogram;
- asking a hard-nosed boss for a raise;
- initiating conversation with a stranger;
- swimming in shark-infested waters to save someone;
- signing the contract to purchase a home;
- saying "No thank you, I choose not to drink";
- shopping on the day before Christmas;
- going on a diet;

- refusing to "fudge" on your income tax forms;
- venturing into the "combat zone" of a Southern California freeway.

Concerning the last of these, those of us who are targets for urban hunters deserve special recognition. Perhaps a bonus on our paychecks. It's only fair. After all, soldiers receive additional compensation for being shot at on the front line!

I had to smile when I saw this sign:

SOUTHERN CALIFORNIA FREEWAY SCHEDULE

If you're planning a trip to Southern California, please arm yourself according to the schedule below. Failure to comply will suspend you from freeway use, and sentence you to hereafter ride on an L.A. Transit District bus.

Monday	Small arms only—0.38 caliber and under
Tuesday	Ladies' Shotgun Day
Wednesday	Men's Large Caliber—Scoped rifles only
Thursday	Automatic Weapons Day
Friday	Cannon and Bazooka Day— Hand grenades OK mornings only
Saturday	Men's and Women's Open—Competition for prizes (Most cars, highest total value, etc.)
Sunday	Gun Cleaning Day—Off Day (Slingshots, Squirt guns, Threatening gestures)

SOUTHERN CALIFORNIA FREEWAY AUTHORITY
(800) SUR-SHOT

L.A./Long Beach	(213) TAR-GETS
San Fernando Valley	(818) BUL-LETS
Orange County	(714) HAND-GUN
San Diego	(619) WEA-PONS[3]

---

3. Source unknown.

Never would I discount the numerous courageous responses that we continuously make. But there are particular times that especially stand out. Times when we responded to great challenges in ways that surprised even ourselves.

The Scare of a Lifetime

The scene is Israel. The event is a recent Pepperdine University Anthropological Study Tour that my wife and I conducted.

The students were rambunctious. One might even term them daredevils. At a time when the Lebanese were continuously sending bombs into northern Israel (one blew out the side of the bus ahead of ours), these guys pleaded to cross the Lebanese border!

Some walked precariously close to fields in the desert that were filled with unexploded shells. Others leaned over the side of a deep cavern in Jericho.

One day our bus driver, Schlomo, drove us to Masada, the high, flat-topped mountain that overlooks the Dead Sea. The fortress on top of the peak was built by Herod the Great, and is notorious as the locale of the Jews' last stand against the Romans in A.D. 73.[4]

---

4. Masada looms bleak and ominous on the skyline. Rising steeply to 1,300 feet above the Dead Sea, it is topped by a broad plateau of 20 acres.

Here sat Herod's magnificent pleasure palace, with hanging gardens, swimming pool, an elaborate bathhouse, vast stores, a synagogue, and ritual baths—all protected by sentry towers set at intervals along an encircling wall.

After the fall of Jerusalem in A.D. 70, a group of 960 Jewish zealots—men, women, and children—barricaded themselves on Masada and held it for three years. When conquest seemed imminent and the Romans were ready to burst in, Josephus tells us that the commander, Eleazar ben Yair, spoke to the defenders, enjoining each man to kill his family, then they "chose ten men by lot to slay all the rest . . . and when these ten had slain them all, they made the same rule for casting lots for themselves." (Wars of the Jews, book VII: 9:1)

When the Romans eventually entered, they found ample stores to show it was not lack of provisions that caused the Jews to surrender; otherwise they found nothing but piles of corpses and a deathly silence.

Few experiences are more moving than being present at a ceremony on the summit of Masada, when the new recruits to the Parachute Division of Israel's Defense Army take their oath of allegiance to the state and solemnly swear that "Masada shall not fall again!"

Sylvia Mann, This Is Israel (Herzlia, Israel: Palphot Ltd., 1980), pp. 83-87.

Our guide, Money Ravid, was thirtyish and sported a bright-colored orange beanie. He was a bit of a know-it-all. All the way to Masada he spoke of the glamorous site that awaited us, with its breath-taking view from the top.

We became more excited by the moment. The risk-loving students sported their climbing clothes; they intended to scale the heights. I assumed that our verbose guide would lead them.

But Money turned out to be a wimp. When the bus reached the foot of the mountain's treacherous cliffs, he announced that he would *not* be climbing. Instead, he would be riding the cable car to the top.

Well, he had me painted into a corner. I wasn't about to let my danger-loving students go alone. It was up to me to go with them. Reluctantly, I announced my intentions.

By now, you'd think that our guide would have nothing more to say. Not so. He looked at me and declared, "Last week, I came here and climbed Masada with a fellow younger than you and in great condition. Halfway up he collapsed with a heart attack and died. The heat must have gotten to him."

His motormouth refused to stop. "Do you realize how easy it is to slip off the treacherous Snake Path when you're delirious with heat?" Yes, I had some idea, and realized that it would be well over 100 degrees today.

I almost backed out then and there but knew that our gang would never let me forget it. I had to go through with this insane mission, leaving our Coke-sipping, smart-cracking, rested guide behind, with my wife and a few of the girls.

We began the climb. At first it was a snap. The students joked, sang, and goofed-off. But that was before it became very steep. And the trail became much more narrow.

Everyone became quiet, as their faces reflected the tremendous strain and the torturous temperature.

The girl behind me suddenly slipped on some loose gravel. But she miraculously managed to stop herself at the cliff's edge. She muttered to herself: "Well, you almost ate the big one." Although it was college student jargon, I didn't have to ask what she meant.

As I was helping her recover, someone pointed upward and yelled. It was Money, my wife, and the girls going overhead in the cable car. They yelled out some taunting remarks. For them the ride was no more frightening than a day trip to Disneyland!

We kept trudging along. Slipping. Sliding. Straining. When I began to feel more confident about our chances of making it, one of the heartiest members of the group suddenly stopped and clutched a large boulder. He was obviously hyperventilating and perhaps even in the throes of a heat stroke. We stopped to provide some shade and liquid. He finally responded. We started climbing once again. Again this young man was stricken.

This went on for the remainder of the way.

Other students were looking very peaked and dizzy. More were slipping now, and some were scaring themselves by looking down. Looking over the edge of that high trail gave me the sensation of being on the tip of an airplane wing while in flight.

At last the end came. We had made it to the top. And with no casualties. Those awaiting us at the top let out a cheer and rushed to us with refreshing drinks. Money just shook his head, sighed, and looked the other way.

But we didn't care. We had made it—in spite of our fears, the heat, the steepness, and everything else. And we proudly walked over together and bought T-shirts boasting "I climbed Masada."

To some who have endured far more, our feat might seem very insignificant, but to us it seemed like a very courageous adventure. In my case, it was an adventure forced upon me, but it was an adventure nevertheless.

We had experienced firsthand the tremendous exhilaration that accompanies beating the odds, challenging the difficult, surmounting the fears—and claiming the victory.

Did we manifest authentic courage? It sure felt like it. But was it really? Let's focus on the intricate meanings associated with this honored virtue. To do so might encourage all of us to "climb many Masadas" in our future lives.

A Quality That Distinguishes

The Random House Dictionary defines "courage" as: "the ability to face difficulty or danger with firmness and without fear."[5]

Allow me to edit that definition to read: "The ability and commitment to *endure and challenge* difficulty or danger with firmness *in spite of* fear."

For purposes of clarification, let's contrast courage with some other concepts that are often confused with it.

First, courage is not the same as *"impulsive reaction."* The latter is a knee-jerk response that occurs without serious reflection or reference to moral principles. Usually it consists of rapid retaliation for perceived threat.

To fly off the handle in a fit of rage is neither commendable nor courageous. It betrays a basic weakness of character.

Honk at slow drivers. Yell at an unfair boss. Slap a disobedient child. Cuss out a waitress who spills hot coffee on your new suit. Some may see these behaviors as courageous. Don't believe them for a minute. These actions reveal a real problem. An ocean of distance exists between such infantile reactions and the real McCoy.

Second, courage is certainly not synonymous with *indifference to ear, pain, or stress.*

The most courageous persons are those who have hearts that pound like muffled drums, and fears that soar, yet they still walk resolutely into the jaws of trial and danger. For them, encounter is a purposive and conscious choice, rather than an attempt to deny reality.

My experience as a marriage counselor attests to the fact that most divorces occur because one or both partners attempt to block out fear, pain, or stress. They engage in continual denial, gingerly sidestepping their problems. As a result their psychic "gunnysacks" begin to fill—and finally break.

How much better it would be to air grievances, to admit pain, to talk over fears. Granted, that requires true courage—especially when it involves close intimates.

---

5. *The Random House Dictionary,* Jess Stein, Editor in Chief (New York: Ballantine Books, n.d.), p. 211.

Courage is light-years away from denial. Rather, it suggests the opposite.

Finally, courage is not necessarily synonymous with *"heroic action."* For one thing, the former involves more "being" than "doing." Here the focus is on inner character: values, priorities, mind-set, attitudes, commitments.

To be open to new ways of thinking requires courage, as does developing personal maturity and sensitivity. For many, achieving self-honesty is more difficult than fighting in wars.

Certainly, courage will involve action. Once we develop an inner boldness, based on conviction rather than expediency, we will take courageous action. Action that sets us off from the crowd and makes us independent of its approval. Action that is in harmony with the inner selves we have created.

Will such action be perceived as "heroic"? Not usually.

Recently, a lady ran her car into a lake behind our house. A youth who witnessed the whole thing, tore off his shoes and dived in. After a great struggle, he freed the lady and brought her to the surface. His response to a reporter is typical of a courageous person.

Reporter: "Do you see yourself as a hero?"

Boy: "Not in the least. I simply responded the way any responsible person should have."

If we're courageous, we'll constantly be involved in similar—but far less dramatic—actions. Returning lost money. Telling it straight to an alcoholic friend. Voting our conscience. Standing with a powerless person who has been wronged by another.

On second thought, perhaps some of these do border on the heroic.

Refuse to Be Tricked!

As we have seen, courage must be separated from facsimiles and counterfeits. This is the first step in gaining a full appreciation of, and desire for, the real thing.

As long as we buy into a caricature of this essential quality, we will fail to absorb it into our lives.

Once again, courage does not mean impulsively, instantly,

avenging every wrong or correcting every inaccuracy. Often the most courageous action is to patiently wait for the right time and opportunity.

Likewise, fear, pain, and stress are about as likely to disappear as California earthquakes and Texas flash floods. And with as much warning! They are trials that must be borne by all.

But make no mistake about it, the courageous person is better able to cope. Why? Because he is able to change fear, pain, and stress from liabilities and depressors into assets and motivators.

As for heroics, we must realize that most courage issues forth in quiet, unnoticed, and unappreciated ways. No brass bands. No newspaper accolades. No medals of honor. Just the inner satisfaction that comes with realizing that courage is its own reward. It does wonders for ourselves and for anyone else who chooses to notice.

Abraham Lincoln once said, "My purpose in living is to plant a flower where a weed once grew." If enough of us plant "flowers of courage," our world will be a much better place!

There is more to understand about this marvelous virtue. Once we distinguish it from its counterfeits, we must explore its many forms. Let's see how many of these we possess and which of them are closely related to Christian discipleship.

CHAPTER THREE

A Lot Like Ice Cream

"It's not that I'm afraid to die, I just don't want to be there when it happens." (Woody Allen)

"I cannot praise a fugitive and cloistered virtue, unexercised and unbreathed, that never sallies out and sees her adversity, but slinks out of the race where that immortal garland is to be run for, not without dust and heat." (John Milton)

"If you stop and ask yourself why you are not so devoted as the (early) Christians, your own heart will tell you that it is neither through ignorance nor inability, but purely because you never thoroughly intended it." (William Law)

There are as many kinds of courage as there are flavors of ice cream. And, like that favorite summertime dessert, they all seem to be extremely appealing.

We've heard numerous synonymns for courage. Among them: backbone, grit, mettle, heart, spunk, and daring.

Likewise, cliches related to the virtue extend from sea to shining sea. Run the gauntlet. Bell the cat. Take the bull by the horns. Beard the lion in his den. Take heart. Keep your chin up—and a stiff upper lip. Stand the gaff. Stick to your guns.

Though similar in meaning, these references to boldness highlight a rich panorama of different perspectives. We are well-advised to scrutinize the various shades of meaning, in order to fully comprehend this universally-revered virtue.

Though classifications are quite arbitrary, for the sake of

clarification, let us state that courage seems to exist in five basic forms. We'll briefly explore each of them.

1. Fortitude

Obviously, in all of us, the physical (kinetic) is closely interrelated with the mental (cognitive) and emotional (cathectic). Nevertheless, there is a brand of courage that is calculated to cause extreme discomfort to our bodies. Some call it "moxie"; I call it "fortitude."

To "bite the bullet," and take punishing licks, is a form of courage that is especially associated with athletes.

Ready for a baseball trivia question? Who is Clint Courtney?

If you're unsure, don't bother requesting the answer from Cooperstown, N.Y. Clint never came close to making it into the Baseball Hall of Fame. In fact, it's very doubtful that his picture appeared on any bubble gum cards.

This guy wasn't a legend in his own time—not even in his own mind. He was only a memory maker for his family, and a few die-hard fans who were inspired by his tremendous fortitude.

Clint played catcher for the Baltimore Orioles in the 1950s. During his career he earned the nickname of Scrap Iron, implying that he was hard, weathered, tough.

Old Scrap broke no records—only bones. He had little power or speed on the base paths. As for grace and style, he made the easiest play look rather difficult. But armed with mitt and mask, Scrap Iron never flinched from any challenge.

Batters often missed the ball and caught his shin. Their foul tips nipped his elbow. Runners fiercely plowed into him, spikes first, as he defended home plate.

Though often doubled over in agony, and flattened in a heap of dust, Clint Courtney never quit. Invariably, he'd slowly get up, shake off the dust, punch the pocket of his mitt once, twice, and nod to his pitcher to throw another one.

The game would go on and Courtney with it—scarred, bruised, clutching his arm in pain, but determined to continue.

He resembled a POW with tape, splints, braces, and other kinds of paraphernalia that wounded people wear. Some made fun of him—calling him a masochist. Insane. Others remember him as a true champion.

Like many of the other kinds of courage, this type of courage can be carried to the extreme. But it seems as if Scrap Iron's approach to baseball should be our approach to life's game. We're thrown many curve balls, take our blows, and endure plenty of unexpected losses.¹ But when the dust clears we must somehow stagger to our feet and invite life's next pitch.

1. Fortitude
2. Bravery

Although it may overlap into several of the other areas, the kind of courage that responds to a crisis is termed "bravery." And it is best understood by focusing on a real-life drama.

A heavy, swirling snowstorm had choked Washington, D.C.'s streets on this frigid January morning in 1982. Fourteenth Street Bridge, spanning the Potomac River, resembled a parking lot. Suddenly, a blue, green, and white jetliner broke out of the opaque sky, losing altitude and heading straight for the crowded bridge.

Motorists gasped in horror as the doomed aircraft raked the surface of the northbound span, sheared tops off several cars, then plunged into the icy waters as it broke apart.

Air Florida's flight 90, a Boeing 737 bound for Tampa, had crashed with 79 people aboard. Only five would survive.

Though unreachable, victims were still visible under rescue workers' lights. Trapped in their seat belts in the split and sunken fuselage, they were slowly covered by the river's ice.

Paramedic Gene Windsor maneuvered his helicopter dangerously close to the water's surface, as he towed the few survivors to shore with a lifeline. The craft's skids could have iced, which might have caused him to lose control.

Truly, his bravery was exemplary. But there were others like him.

One woman, 22-year-old Priscilla Tirado, lost her grip on

---

1. "Old Scrap Iron," by Diane Cole, *Psychology Today*, May 1988, p. 66ff.

the rope, and was on the verge of drowning. An onlooker, Lenny Skutnik, suddenly plunged in and—risking his life—he saved hers. A medical exam revealed that Priscilla's body temperature was so low, that she was only a few minutes from death by cardiac arrest.

But there was another gentleman, Arland D. Williams, whose bravery was especially heartwarming.

He was among the six who clung to the aircraft's tail—waiting for the helicopter to pull them to shore. According to witnesses, Mr. Williams repeatedly passed the lifeline to the others rather than grabbing onto it himself.

When the chopper finally returned for him, he had slipped beneath the surface. With reverence, Windsor later said: "I've never seen one man with that much commitment."[2]

What a sharp contrast with a scene that occurred on a New York street nearly two decades before. Kitty Genovese was slowly and brutally stabbed to death. At least thirty-eight of her neighbors witnessed the attack and heard her screams.

In the course of the 90-minute episode, her attacker was actually frightened away, then he returned to finish her off. Yet not once during that period did any neighbor assist her, or even telephone the police.[3]

---

2. "Death on the Potomac," no author stated, *Newsweek*, January 25, 1982, p. 26.

Lenny Skutnik and Arland D. Williams were cited, in President Ronald Reagan's "State of the Union Address" in January of 1982, as special examples of American courage. Furthermore, the U.S. Coast Guard presented Arland D. Williams the Lifesaving Medal posthumously, on June 6, 1983, in a White House Rose Garden ceremony. (Information received by the office of former President, Ronald Reagan, in Los Angeles, California in July 1989.)

3. The implications of this tragic event shocked America, and it stimulated two young psychologists, Darley and Latane, to study the conditions under which people are or are not willing to help others in an emergency. In essence, they concluded that responsibility is diffused.

The more people present in an emergency situation, the less likely it is that any one of them will offer help. This is popularly called the "bystander effect."

(In the actual experiment, when one bystander was present, 85 percent offered help. When two were present, 62 percent offered help. When five were present, then it decreased to 31 percent.)

Lawrence S. Wrightsman, *Social Psychology in the Seventies* (Monterey, Calif.: Brooks/Cole Publishing Company, 1972), pp. 33-34.

The bravery displayed in the Washington event makes us rejoice in our humanity. We stand tall. But the scenario in New York, with its vivid display of cowardice, causes us to feel sorrow and shame.

Certainly, bravery is a kind of courage that we need to see frequently. It is essential for our nation, for our communities, and for our homes.

1. Fortitude
2. Bravery
3. Valor

When courage is transferred to the battlefield, it is referred to as valor. Though similar, in many respects, to the kinds of courage we have already discussed, valor is motivated by these added dimensions: intense patriotism, accentuated morale, extreme conformity, and a great feeling of teamwork—even with those at home.

One more thing. Soldiers infused with valor tend to be very optimistic about their chances for victory.

In a speech to Pepperdine students, Los Angeles Dodger manager Tommy Lasorda declared that George Custer had to be the greatest optimist who ever lived.

Evidence? Before charging into the Battle of Little Bighorn, he yelled these words to his soldiers: "Don't take any prisoners!"

Now that's real optimism.

As a boy in Hattiesburg, Mississippi, I vividly recall the return of a wartime hero. His name: Henry A. Commisky. With thousands of other people and brass bands, I greeted the white-uniformed, smiling hero.

Every kid in the city jammed into the Community Center to hear the words of this Korean War hero. He began by telling us what he had done.

His entire unit had been ambushed by machine guns. In the hail of bullets he rushed to overtake one of the mounted weapons, wheeled it around, and shot scores of communist soldiers.

He had saved his unit and even forced the enemy to retreat.

His advice to us, as we sat there hanging on his every word: "Kids, just remember one thing. Never stop playing with your toy guns, and you may become a hero too."

I always knew there was a deep, profound purpose to all the squirt gun fights we had in the neighborhood!

Well, our town gave Henry and his bride a new "house of his dreams." It seemed a small reward for his valor. He was a war hero par excellence.

Nice story. Great ending. But, to be candid, valor can get out of hand. Who hasn't grimaced at the gory details of the My Lai incident—when Lt. Calley and his regiment killed and mutilated scores of innocent Vietnamese citizens.[4] A clear case of what social psychologists often term "overobedience."

Perhaps every virtue, including valorous courage, when pushed to its extreme becomes a vice. If so, Christian military personnel must be on guard.

With good reason, we turn to the next kind of courage to offer such a balance—a balance that emerges from an enlightened and sensitive conscience.

1. Fortitude
2. Bravery
3. Valor
4. Resoluteness

There is a kind of courage that is based on inner conviction. It springs forth from a deep commitment to some moral principle. As a result, a resolution is made to tenaciously fight (or endure) for that belief.

Here again, this distinction is a matter of focus. The spotlight is on a strongly held value. And all, even one's life, is subordinated to the latter. Perhaps the Reverend Martin Luther King, Jr. was referring to resoluteness when he penned: "A person is not prepared to live, unless there is a cause for which he is ready to die."

---

4. Lt. Calley resorted to sadism, as did many under his command. It is known, for instance, that he sent out Christmas cards with a picture of a large stack of dead "enemies."

The same Dr. King pointed to a shining example of this virtue. He once described this woman as "the great fuse that led to the modern stride toward freedom." But, in actuality, she made that stride while sitting still. Let me relate her inspiring story.

There is about this woman no aura of distinction. There is about her dress and manner no commanding uniqueness. Yet her story is one of the most inspirational to emerge from the civil rights movement.

On the evening of December 1, 1955 Rosa Parks caught the Cleveland Avenue bus to return home from her job as a seamstress. She knew that the ride would take 15 minutes, so she leaned back to relax.

Soon the bus filled to capacity. The white bus driver noticed that this black woman was occupying a seat in the "white" section—while a white passenger was standing. Yelling out, he ordered the "offender" to the rear.

Now Rosa wasn't one to defy authority. She was no rabble-rousing integrationist. Just a simple, forty-year-old garment worker who wanted to rest after a hard day's labor.

But in Rosa's mind, the bus driver had violated a basic moral principle. Granted, he had the law behind him, but it still didn't seem right. So Rosa remained seated.

In so doing, she didn't make a scene, no screams, no whines, no threats. She simply didn't move—thus forcing those who wanted to force her to move to make the next move.

The frightened black lady was arrested, jailed, and brought to trial. A twenty-six-year-old minister, Dr. King, heard about the case. On December 5, he urged Montgomery's blacks to boycott the bus system. They did.

How did the episode end? Buses were desegregated the following year, and the era of passive resistance began that culminated in the signing of the civil rights acts of the 1960s.

Mrs. Parks paid dearly for her courage. Her husband, a barber, became ill from the stress. The family was forced to move to Detroit. Mrs. Parks had to do sewing and alterations at home.

Today she is active in youth work, job guidance, and cultural and recreational planning for her people. In addition, she serves as a deaconess of St. Matthew's African Methodist Episcopal Church in Detroit. For her past and present contributions she is greatly revered.

What was the inner resolution she had, and resolutely defended? Very simply, she strongly believed that human dignity cannot interminably be undermined by brute force. And it wasn't![5]

The Upward Spiral

The foregoing courage types overlap, and are certainly not an exhaustive list. Yet they seem to be among the most noteworthy and frequently evidenced aspects of courage in our world.

Each mentioned is commendable in its own right. Nevertheless, in the thinking of this author, the order in which they are presented suggests the ascending order of their value—from fortitude to resoluteness. But most of us are grateful for courage, however, whenever, and wherever it has existed. Sure, some forms of courage have been badly misdirected, but most have been of great benefit to mankind.

Like Charles Swindoll, I'm glad that some very special persons refused to take the easy way. Refused to listen to the advice of quitters, pessimists, doomsayers, and wet blankets.

I'm glad, for example:

- that *Edison* didn't give up on the light bulb, even though his helpers seriously doubted that the thing would ever work;
- that *Luther* refused to back down when the church doubled her fists and clenched her teeth;
- that *Michelangelo* kept pounding and painting; regardless of the pope's negative put-downs;
- that *Lindbergh* decided to fly the ocean blue, when everyone else said it was ridiculous and dangerous;

---

5. *The Negro Almanac: A Reference Work on the Afro-American,* ed. Harry A. Ploski and James Williams (New York: John Wiley and Sons, 1983), pp. 31, 228, 1325-26.

- that *Father ten Boom* said yes to frightened Jews who needed a hiding place;
- that Julliard School of Music saw past leg braces and a wheelchair to admit an unlikely violin student named *Perlman.*[6]

We could add to this list. We might deserve to be on, or greatly desire to be on, the list ourselves. If so, we're to be commended.

But it is crucial that we not stop, nor even linger, in our quest for courage. There is one more kind of courage to consider. Without a doubt, it is far superior to any types that we've mentioned—and often includes them.

Furthermore, we need not awkwardly grope for this prize. There is One who has led the way and desires to lead *our* way. His name is Jesus. In a real way, it seems like He invented courage—having relinquished heaven to face such opposition on earth.

Let's closely examine this final form of courage by going to the source. For it is in His character that this form is best revealed.

To do so will be to draw strength, receive guidance, and commit ourselves to the special type of courage that made Him so triumphant.

For it is the same kind that distinguishes us as His followers.

6. Charles R. Swindoll, *The Quest for Character* (Portland, Ore.: Multnomah Press, 1967), pp. 134-5.

SECTION TWO

COURAGE:
Why Is It So Essential for Christians?

CHAPTER FOUR

O Holy Knight

People are much like tea bags. You never know their real strength until they get in hot water!

"Some men see things that are and ask 'Why?'; but I see things that never have been and ask 'why not?'" *(George Bernard Shaw)*

The life that we have is our gift from *God; what we do with that life is our gift* to *God.*

A popular writer declares: "Our Lord Jesus held nothing back when He left heaven, lived on earth, and went for it—all the way to the Cross—and beyond."[1]

Did Christ have courage? Do lions roar? Is Alaska cold in winter? He "wrote the book" on courage, and it contains all four forms we've discussed.

Fortitude? How else can we explain His serenity in the boat, with panic-stricken disciples, during the tumultuous storm? (Luke 8:22-25)

Bravery? The number of crises He faced resemble the airplanes stacked up in holding patterns over Chicago. They arrived one after another and often simultaneously!

He lovingly intervened for the demon-possessed (Mark 5:1-20), lepers (Luke 5:12-14), hungry (John 6:5-14), deaf (Mark 7:31-35), and even the dead (Luke 8:49-56).

---

1. Charles R. Swindoll, *The Quest for Character* (Portland, Ore.: Multnomah Press, 1987), p. 135.

Valor? Granted, our Lord wore no military uniform. But He waged continuous war against assaulting armies; the scribes and Pharisees (Mark 7:1-16); moneychangers in the temple, along with the wicked chief priests who supported them (11:15-18); and even a "lynch mob" (Luke 4:16-30).

Resoluteness? Our Saviour clearly articulated support for righteous, though unpopular, principles. His Sermon on the Mount was revolutionary—cutting cross-grain against this world's value system (Matt. 5–7). Another time, when He healed on the Sabbath and declared His equality with His Father, the Jews threatened His life (John 5:1-18).

A biting rebuke of lawyers issued forth from His lips: "Woe to you because you load people down with burdens they can hardly carry, and you yourselves will not lift one finger to help them" (Luke 11:46).

Nor were His disciples spared. He chastised them for rebuking little children (Matt. 19:13-14), not having enough faith to cast out demons (Mark 9:18-19), and conspiring to obtain positions of power (Matt. 20:20-28).

Jesus possessed all of these forms of courage: fortitude, bravery, valor, and resoluteness. In addition, He manifested a fifth quality of courage that transcends even these four. For lack of a better term, I shall refer to this quality as "chivalry."

One dictionary defines chivalry as: "the qualities expected of a knight, as courage, generosity, and courtesy . . . gallant[ry] to[ward] women."[2]

Let's see how Jesus is our "Holy Knight."

1. Fortitude
2. Bravery
3. Valor
4. Resoluteness
5. Chivalry
Add heroism to the four kinds of courage discussed in the last chapter. Then combine heroism with gallantry, courtesy, and a

---

2. *The Random House Dictionary,* Jess Stein, editor in chief (New York: Ballantine Books, 1980), p. 160.

gentle graciousness toward the weak and helpless. The whole package suggests chivalry—a word that originates from the days of medieval knighthood.

The imagery is refreshing to ponder. We visualize troops of brave men carrying brightly-colored banners, riding forth to protect the weak, maintain righteousness, and uphold justice.

Women were special objects of the knights' care. By defending women, and all who were at the mercy of the brute powers of a barbaric world, knights won for themselves a shining place in history. And they gave chivalry a splendor that will never fade.

Jesus of Nazareth embodied the best of knightly virtues. He journeyed forth, "clad in armor of a peerless manhood," to shield the defenseless, promote the holy, and reveal a sacrificial life that would inspire the world. He stands forever as the Knight of knights.[3]

In what specific ways was our Lord chivalrous? Let's look at five scenes, as though they were color slides, that reveal some idea of the depths of his fathomless courage.

Water Shared by Brothers

Scene number one: The Jordan River.

There appeared to be little reason for Jesus to go through with this ritual. His heart was unstained by sin, and John's baptism was one of repentance.

Furthermore, His participation might lead to misunderstanding. How would the opened sky, the dove, and the voice from heaven be interpreted by those present? Indeed, there were great risks involved.

John even did his best to dissuade Jesus.

But Jesus went through with it. Why? Because He desired to intimately identify with His sinful countrymen—to climb down into the trenches with them and share their experiences firsthand.

Though sinless, Jesus began His ministry by linking Himself

---

3. Charles Edward Jefferson, chapter XIV entitled "His Chivalry," *The Character of Jesus* (New York: Grosset and Dunlap, 1908), pp. 171-185.

with those who endured the burden of transgression, and cried out for deliverance (Mark 1:1-11). And that began a pattern that lasted until the end of His earthly sojourn. Unlike many Christians today, never was He satisfied with keeping sinners at arm's length. Instead, His arms embraced them tightly.

Why? Let's hear His answer to some Pharisees. They had heard how Jesus dined with Matthew—a man of questionable character at the time. So they asked His disciples, "Why does your teacher eat with tax collectors and sinners?"

Overhearing the question, He answered: "It is not the healthy who need a doctor, but the sick . . . I have not come to call the righteous, but sinners" (Matt. 9:12-13).

Jesus expects us to come out from behind cloistering church walls. Linkage must be made. Significant identification must be established between those of us who are spiritually healthy and have access to the Doctor's medicine (His Word and Presence), and those who are mired in sin.

Palestine's Mayo Clinic

Suffering and physical distress pierced our Lord's heart. And He was well aware of His nation's neglect of the sick.

In Jesus' world there was no Medicare, no health insurance, no hospitals as we know them. Sure, the wealthy could hire trained medical personnel to alleviate pain and lessen the terrors associated with dying. But the poor suffered unattended and died unrelieved.

The mentally disturbed were not properly cared for. On the contrary, they were considered demon-possessed and driven from town. The tragic result: They were forced to live in desolate, uninhabited places—such as deserts and cemeteries. Persons passing by were terrorized by their troubled cries and loud shrieks.

Jesus pitied the possessed. But even more important, He dared to reach out in love. Mark 5 vividly illustrates this conclusion.

Scene number two: a small fishing boat, with Jesus inside, makes its way across the Sea of Galilee to the region of the Gerasenes. A greatly disturbed tomb dweller, with superhuman strength, rushes out to meet Him.

Neither chains nor irons could bind this man — nor did anyone attempt to stifle his blood-curdling cries, or restrain his self-inflicted mutilations made with sharp rocks. He was a ghastly site, and he frightened all — except Jesus.

Worst of all, the disheveled man was so saturated with evil spirits that they became his ventriloquist. He remained silent. They spoke through his mouth and pleaded for mercy, knowing of Christ's power to destroy them.

Jesus expelled the demons into swine, all of which plunged off cliffs into the lake — much to the consternation of their owners.[4]

Then we are shown another picture. There stands a dressed, composed, rational human being. So radically changed was the grave dweller, that those who had known him before were absolutely petrified of the man, and also of our omnipotent Saviour (v. 15).

By the time the story had been disseminated by persons with twisted perspectives, the entire region was in pandemonium. As a result the Great Physician was told to leave their region (v. 17).

Who would ever think that offering relief to a pitiful man would result in rejection? Jesus knew that it would beforehand, but that didn't stop Him. He went straight ahead and followed His agenda of love. That took courage. Lots of it.

Jesus regretted what He had done about as much as the man He had "resurrected." Forgive my "loose cannon conjecture," but as His boat slid off the sand onto the lake, I can imagine my Lord smiling and saying to Himself, "It's unfortunate about all those pigs, but those Gentiles shouldn't be eating all that bacon anyway."

---

4. In May 1987, I crossed over to the northeastern side of the Sea of Galilee, to the place thought to be the exact site of this story. My student, Bo Cassell, and I climbed the mountain to visualize how the event might have occurred.

There are open fields where the pigs might have been kept. At the western side of the fields were cliffs overlooking the water. Evidently, these were the very cliffs from which the pigs hurled themselves. The ruins of an ancient church were just below us, marking the site and commemorating the miracle.

Strictly Generic; Definitely Not Designer!

Between Galilee and Judea lived people, half-Jewish and half-pagan, who had morally degenerated from the high ideals of earlier days. Jews referred to these Samaritans as apostates and treated them like lepers.

Rarely would a true Hebrew journey through that defiled land. *Scene number three,* however, reveals the Good Shepherd not only passing through, but lingering to minister to His sheep—just as He did with the Judeans and Galileans.

No man could intimately socialize with Samaritans without paying a great price. Jesus paid it. People gnashed their teeth and hissed: "You are a Samaritan" (John 8:48). In their minds, this was the most derogatory thing they could possibly say, but it didn't cause Christ to lose heart or to be diverted from His mission.

He healed Samaritans and pointed them to God. Though the rabbis considered them to be outcasts, and banned them from temple ceremonies, Jesus warmly took them in.

In fact, when He offered a parable that depicted His model for true righteousness, its star was a Samaritan. Today, we know it as the story of the "Good Samaritan." Not incidentally, the villains are portrayed as Jewish ecclesiastical bureaucrats (Luke 10:30-37).

One of the most chivalrous things anyone can possibly do is confront entrenched prejudice. People who champion the cause of the attacked are frequently made targets of abuse. But the Knight of Galilee unflinchingly pursued His course. His heavenly "marching orders" included taking a stand for these abandoned, hopeless people. And He obeyed—which was His style.

Woman: Animal, Vegetable, or Mineral?

Like all true knights, it is in His treatment of women that Christ's chivalry reaches its highest expression.

In His part of the world, females were not treated fairly. They were never perceived as being equal to men.

Jesus boldly defended the women of His day. He attacked divorce laws, which put women at the mercy of men. The latter could abandon their wives simply by signing a statement of declaration.

This was an open-eyed, defiant misrepresentation of Moses' Law. Jesus knew it. They knew it. Jesus knew that they knew it, and it made them angry. Our Lord proclaimed the principle of "indissolubility," in relationship to marriage. One marriage for life. Period (Matt. 5:27-32).

In those days adulterous men went about scot-free. Not so with women. Those caught were stoned. One such person was dragged to Jesus in an attempt to entrap Him. Would He obey Mosaic Law, and advise that she be destroyed, or would He declare another of His "heresies"?

They received their answer that day—an extremely courageous answer which pointed a finger at the accusers. Result: a forgiven and very relieved woman went her way—and some embarrassed men stormed away with guilt and anger (John 8:3-11).

Scene four: Jacob's Well. The place where Jesus offers the ultimate example of His respect for womanhood.

It was here that He was nonkosher in three ways. He spoke to a woman in public. She was a "despicable" Samaritan. To compound His "crime" even further, she happened to be an overachiever when it came to blatant fornication. Talk about questionable credentials. A good Jew certainly wouldn't give her the time of day!

But Jesus gave her more than that; He offered her eternal life. He did it without condescending or insulting. And why not? It's exactly what we would expect this Holy Knight to do.

It can safely be said that no person who has walked this earth did more for women than our Lord. He treated them like real people—not toys, or animals, or even like subordinate humans. Christ regarded women as bona fide, genuinely equal human beings.

As impressive as Christ's treatment of women is, I hasten to reveal *scene number five.* In many ways, it demonstrates His chivalry more than any other instance. It occurs somewhere at the base of Mount Hermon in northern Palestine— perhaps near Caesarea Philippi.

The Galvanized Gaze

To speak up for a noble cause is commendable. To offer a compassionate heart and a helping hand to the helpless is admirable. But the highest expression of chivalry is offering to die for others. John's Gospel states, "Greater love has no one than this, that one lay down his life for his friends" (John 15:13).

Jesus was neither a sick masochist, nor One who dreamed of posthumous headlines of grandeur. He was not even caught up in the kind of battle psychology which causes men to throw themselves into enemy fire. Rather, He calmly, clear-mindedly, and compassionately chose to give His life for the greatest cause ever—eternal life.

Capture the setting. (Luke 9) Our Lord had just come from His glorious Transfiguration on Mount Hermon (vv. 28-36). Peter, James, and John were there to witness His translucent face and clothes. They also saw Moses and Elijah—the greatest lawgiver and the greatest prophet—appear before their shocked eyes.

Why did these saints make an appearance? To talk about His soon approaching death (v. 31b) and primarily to offer encouragement to the Lamb who would shortly be slain for many. In essence, it was a "Come on, You can do it!" pep talk.

Well, down the mountain came Jesus and the three disciples—only to be met by a convulsing, demon-possessed child whom the other disciples had been unable to help. Exasperated, Jesus called them an "unbelieving and perverse generation." Then He healed the grateful lad.

While the crowd marveled, our Lord turned to the disciples and said, "Listen carefully to what I am about to tell you. The Son of Man is going to be betrayed into the hands of men" (v. 44). Unfortunately He received no sympathy nor even understanding. "They did not grasp it, and they were afraid to ask Him about it" (v. 45).

It was like they were saying, "Look, don't dump this depressing thought on us now. Besides, what you're talking about is over our heads." I'm reminded of the saying: There is none so blind as he who *will not* see.

These same disciples begin arguing over which of them was the greatest. Jesus slowly reached out to grasp the hand of a child and snuggled him to His breast, saying, "He who is least among you all—he is the greatest" (v. 48). Case closed. Almost.

John began to tattle on someone, a man who had successfully driven out demons in the Master's name. His big sin? "He is not one of us" (v. 49). This man was a believer, no doubt, but not one of the pedigreed—not one of the twelve "biggies." Kindly but firmly, Jesus offered John a lesson on tolerance.

The Transfiguration had been awesome. Though the subject discussed was His death, the Transfiguration provided a real uplift. And yet we see these three stark examples of sin and immaturity in the lives of the ones He had gently taught for so long.

Must He die for these and their faithless generation?

You bet. For every last one of them. From the most righteous and obedient follower to the most heinous criminal— both of whom He met on Calvary.

Verse 51 is cryptic in its imagery: And so, "Jesus resolutely set out for Jerusalem." He faced the music. He gazed at the tragedy that lay before Him, and intentionally took the first step toward that destination.

In so doing, He agreed to endure the events which are now so familiar to us. Betrayals. Scourgings. Jeers. False accusations. Pain too intense to imagine. He looked ahead and saw it all in vivid, excruciating detail.

But His face remained set in that direction. He was not looking back like Lot's wife (Gen. 19:23-26; Luke 17:30-33), not second-guessing like Elijah under the juniper tree (1 Kings 19:3-9), and not attempting to maneuver or sidestep. He did not plead "special case status" like those who disdain military conquest; He did not delay.

No, our Lord set His face resolutely toward Jerusalem. Though He reached out for added strength and confirmation in the Garden of Gesthemane, He never cowered or flinched a muscle until He reached the cross. Picture Him as He courageously marches onward:

"... trampling on all the precious things on earth, putting under His feet the ambitions by which the hearts of other men are fired, trampling into the dust the prizes and the joys of life ... Jesus placed every one of them beneath His feet."[5]

A Knight of His God's Heavenly Order

Jesus Christ was chivalrous, like the loyal, courageous, and compassionate knights of old. He shared so many of their graces and virtues. He had nerve, mettle, and the intrepidity of the bravest of knights, together with a winsomeness and divine graciousness which history cannot match.

Yet, it is important to remember that Jesus Christ was the Holy Knight of God's heavenly order—which distinguishes Him from medieval warriors in important ways:

- They primarily sought adventure; His adventure came to Him.
- They clad themselves in metal; His only protection was the white "innocence of an unspoiled heart."
- They possessed the skills of soldiers; His skills were those of a physician.
- They fought to lay their enemies in the dust; His prowess was that of a friend and brother.
- They delighted in pomp and glory; though not in the least bit timid, He shied away from the spotlight of publicity.
- They were ostentatious in style and manner; He went about doing good inconspicuously.
- They protected the distressed and upheld the right but often failed to live stainless lives; He, the Prince of knights and King of all hosts of chivalry, conquered—but lived His life without even the smallest trace of sin![6]

High But Not Out of Reach

When I've heard any of my Lord's virtues extolled, I've often asked myself, *How can I ever hope to reach His example?* Rous-

5. Jefferson, op. cit., pp. 292-293.
6. Ibid., pp. 183-184.

seau was right when he wrote: "If the life and death of Socrates were those of a sage, the life and death of Jesus are those of . . . God."[7]

In a real way my feelings are justified. The creature can forget about approximating the Creator—especially when it comes to having His boldness. Yet, I also realize that resting my case here is a cop-out, one that scores have utilized to sidestep His expectations.

Because God lives in my heart, I do have power—Son-power. I can be bold in faith as I affirm His Presence and tackle challenges that He brings to my attention. I can do this without feeling the least bit arrogant.

Just *how* does this occur, according to God's Word? And *who* are some mortals, like us, who have utilized His power supply to manifest His kind of courage? Our next chapter begins by addressing these questions.

7. Ibid., p. 294.

CHAPTER FIVE

The Significant Insignificant

"Even if you're on the right track, you'll get run over if you just sit there." (Will Rogers)

"Moral courage almost never appears except as part of that greater entity called character." (Allan Nevins)

"Jesus came not to make life easy, but to make men great." (William Barclay)

Who was United States Senator Edmund G. Ross of Kansas? I suppose you could call him a "Mr. Nobody." No law bears his name. Not a single list of Senate "greats" mentions his service.

Yet when Ross entered the Senate in 1866, he was considered the man to watch. He seemed destined to surpass his colleagues, but he tossed it all away by one courageous act of conscience.

Let's set the stage.

Conflict was dividing our government in the wake of the Civil War. President Andrew Johnson was determined to follow Lincoln's policy of reconciliation toward the defeated South. Congress, however, wanted to rule the downtrodden Confederate states with an iron hand.

Congress decided to strike first. Shortly after Senator Ross was seated, the Senate introduced impeachment proceedings against the hated President. The radicals calculated that they needed thirty-six votes, and smiled as they concluded that the thirty-sixth was none other than Ross'.[1]

The new senator listened to the vigilante talk. But to the surprise of many, he declared that the President "deserved as fair a trial as any accused man has ever had on earth."[2] The word immediately went out that his vote was "shaky."

Ross received an avalanche of anti-Johnson telegrams from every section of the country. Radical senators badgered him to "come to his senses."

The fateful day of the vote arrived. The courtroom galleries were packed. Tickets for admission were at an enormous premium.

As a deathlike stillness fell over the Senate chamber, the vote began. By the time they reached Ross, twenty-four "guilties" had been announced. Eleven more were certain. Only Ross' vote was needed to impeach the President.

Unable to conceal his emotion, the Chief Justice asked in a trembling voice, "Mr. Senator Ross, how vote you? Is the respondent Andrew Johnson guilty as charged?"

Ross later explained, at that moment, "I looked into my

---

1. According to John F. Kennedy's account, President Andrew Johnson was convinced that his Secretary of War, Edwin M. Stanton, was seeking to become the "dictator of the south." He asked for his immediate resignation on August 5, 1867. Stanton arrogantly refused to resign until the next meeting of Congress. He was suspended, and General Grant was appointed in his place.

On January 13, a livid Congress notified the President of its displeasure. Grant vacated and Stanton returned—and barricaded himself in his office.

Public sentiment ran heavily against Johnson. He was seen to have intentionally broken the law, and defiantly ignored the will of Congress. Impeachment proceedings began in the House and quickly passed. The trial for his conviction, under the Articles of Impeachment, began on March 5, 1868 in the Senate.

John F. Kennedy, *Profiles in Courage* (New York: Harper and Brothers, Publishers, 1955), pp. 130-131.

2. Senator Jim Lane had preceded Ross. He was sympathetic to President Johnson, and voted to uphold his veto of the Civil Rights Bill of 1866. Radical Kansans held a "kangaroo court" in Lawrence, and soundly condemned the senator. Result: his health broke under the stress and he committed suicide on July 1, 1866.

Ironically, it was the same Edmund G. Ross who introduced the resolutions attacking Lane, who was appointed. The anti-Johnson congressmen were elated, for they "knew where the new senator's loyalties lay." This added to their shock when he finally voted against their wishes (Ibid., p. 129.).

open grave. Friendships, position, fortune, and everything that makes life desirable to an ambitious man were about to be swept away by the breath of my mouth, perhaps forever."

Then, the answer came—unhesitating, unmistakable: "Not guilty!" With that, the trial was over. And the response was as predicted.

A high public official from Kansas wired Ross to say: "Kansas repudiates you as she does all perjurers and skunks."

The "open grave" vision had become a reality. Ross' political career was in ruins. Extreme ostracism, and even physical attack awaited his family upon their return home.

One gloomy day Ross turned to his faithful wife and said, "Millions cursing me today will bless me tomorrow . . . though none but God can know the struggle it has cost me." It was a prophetic declaration.

Twenty years later Congress and the Supreme Court verified the wisdom of his position, by changing the laws related to impeachment.

Ross was appointed Territorial Governor of New Mexico. Then, just prior to his death, he was awarded a special pension by Congress. The press and country took this opportunity to honor his courage which, they finally concluded, had saved our country from crisis and division.[3]

One-Voters, Front-And-Center

My wife sent me a card the other day. On the front it declared, "We didn't make '*Who's Who*' this year." Then, when you opened it, it said, "But we're on page 47 of '*What Was That?*' "

---

3. The Kansas newspapers and political bosses who had soundly denounced Ross two decades before, now praised him for his bold stand against legislative mob rule:

"By the firmness and courage of Senator Ross," it was said, "the country was saved from calamity greater than war, while it consigned him to a political martyrdom, the most cruel in our history. . . . Ross was the victim of a wild flame of intolerance which swept everything before it. He did his duty knowing that it meant his political death.

"It was a brave thing for Ross to do, but Ross did it. He acted for his conscience and with a lofty patriotism, regardless of what he knew must be the ruinous consequences to himself. He acted right" (Ibid., p. 144).

Humbling? You bet. But nevertheless true. Like most people, I consider myself to be a pretty common Joe. A taco-loving, work-resisting, mistake-prone human being. And people like us need to learn lessons from people like us. Does that make sense?

Parade by the greatest political leaders of our past: Washington, Jefferson, Lincoln, Roosevelt. Tell me of their often-repeated acts of courage. I am impressed.

To be honest, however, I'd have to admit that I'm better able to identify with the courage of that lowly senator from Kansas. He had little clout. He had no pedigree. But he *had* one vote and used it wisely. That one vote made a big difference!

If this is so concerning political courage, it is even more true in relation to Christian courage. On one hand, we rejoice in the courageous lives of biblical celebrities—the well-known, enshrined personalities who were gifted with extraordinary talents or positions. To name a few:

- Esther, the beautiful queen;
- David the musical, handsome leader;
- Paul, the captivating speaker;
- John, the graphic revelator.

On the other hand, many of us learn best from the "nobodies" in God's Word— the ones who cast their "one vote." In each case God used that one vote to really make a difference![4]

None of these "nobodies" were considered classy, sharp, or of high calibre; they appeared more *seedy* than *suave*. To many of us, they would seem very insignificant. Underwhelming. Generic saints.

Yet their stories are a tremendous encouragement to us commoners. Why? Because they have somehow made courage seem attainable in our worlds, in spite of our many limitations and liabilities.

---

4. See Jon Johnston, *Christian Excellence: Alternative to Success* (Grand Rapids, Mich.: Baker Book House, 1985), pp. 94-96, for a discussion of little people made big by God. Key point: "God chose (and still chooses) those convinced of their own dependency on Him to confound the proud and powerful; the weak of the world to confound the wise" (Ezek. 17:24; Zech. 4:6).

Let's showcase two of these "significant insignificants"—one from the Old Testament and the other from the New. To do so should give us a couple of "courage transfusions."

A Faith and a Fleece

After forty hard years of wandering in the desert, it was time to invade the Promised Land. In His final prebattle instructions to Joshua, Israel's commander-in-chief, God repeated one phrase three times: "Be strong and *courageous*" (Josh. 1:6).[5]

Perhaps this repetition was necessary. Maybe the leader was hard-of-hearing, senile, or exceedingly nervous. One thing's for sure: Joshua got the message, for he stood strong and courageous during the crucial days that lay ahead.

Joshua sent two spies to Jericho to size up the situation. They ended up at the house of Rahab.[6]

Unfortunately, the city's king knew they were there—and was in hot pursuit. What would Rahab do? Turn them over to the authorities and become a local hero? Or protect them and risk her life? It was a big decision for this lowly innkeeper. But one she had to make quickly.

---

5. Moses has died. Joshua is in command. God instructs him to cross the Jordan and conquer the land, and while doing it, to "be strong and courageous" (Josh. 1:6). To erase all misunderstanding, He says it again: "Be strong and courageous" (v. 7).

After telling him about the importance of keeping the Law, God says, Oh yes, one thing I need to tell you: "Be strong and courageous. Do not be terrified; do not be discouraged, for the Lord your God will be with you wherever you go" (v. 9).

God bids Joshua adieu. The leader turns to instruct his soldiers. Then, after promising to be obedient warriors, they offer Joshua these familiar words, "Only be strong and courageous" (v. 18).

Evidently Joshua got the word—because he was certainly strong and courageous in the important days that followed.

6. The biblical narrative refers to Rahab as a "prostitute." This has caused considerable discussion. Matthew Henry states that she had formerly been of ill repute, had reformed, but could not shed the stigma.

Adam Clarke, on the other hand, contends that harlots and innkeepers were called by the same name. In his words: "I am fully satisfied that the term, 'zonah,' in the text, which has been translated 'harlot,' should be rendered . . . 'inn-keeper' or 'hostess.'"

The *Bethany Parallel Commentary on the Old Testament* (Minneapolis, Minn.: Bethany House Publishers, 1985), p. 394.

Rahab dared to listen to her heart. Having heard of the Red Sea miracle, and Israel's victory over the Amorites, she realized that Jehovah was the true God. She recognized that these were His people, and that they were *her* people!

With a deeply committed faith, she courageously abandoned her security, and did what was necessary to protect the spies.

Rahab took the men to the rooftop and hid them under a stack of flax. When the authorities came to search, Rahab told them that the men had "hit the road." Furthermore, she advised the authorities to chase after the spies. The men liked her idea and were out of there like a flash.

That evening, Rahab revealed her faith to the spies. With heartfelt sincerity, she said, "the Lord your God is God in heaven above and on the earth below" (Joshua 2:11).

Realizing that Israel's forces would be victorious over her city, she then did a very Christian thing. She requested the safety of her family.

The spies were aware that Rahab could still turn them in. She had them over a barrel. So they agreed, but they added some conditions. At the time of the invasion:

1. A scarlet cord (in a sense, a fleece) must be tied in the window, through which they would be escaping.
2. Her relatives must be waiting inside her house.
3. Oh yes, one more thing, the deal was off if she told of their plans.

And with that, the two Israelites were lowered by a rope from the window. After hiding in the hills for three days, they returned to Joshua with their optimistic report and with Rahab's request.

We all know about the famous Battle of Jericho. The walls came down. The city was torched. Every living thing was killed with swords. Correction: *almost* every living thing.

The house bearing the scarlet cord was saved, and Joshua commanded the two spies to "usher" Rahab and her family to a safe place. Furthermore, they were adopted into the Israelite nation (6:20-25).

And that's not all. Not by a long shot. Rahab the "nobody" actually became the ancestress of our Saviour. She married

Salmon, father of Boaz, and became the great-great-grand-mother of King David. Jesus was born of this same lineage, twenty-seven generations later. (See Matthew 1:1-16.)

And to think, all Rahab wanted was to protect her family, to assist those who conquered in the Name of the true God, and to commit her life to Him herself. And God gave her so much more—which is not unlike Him.

Rahab's courageous faith earned her very special recognition in God's Word. The writer of Hebrews declares, "By faith . . . Rahab, because she welcomed the spies, was not killed with those who were disobedient" (Hebrews 11:31).

Impressive! But let's turn our attention to a New Testament "significant insignificant," whose story has made a deep impact on my own life.

Lord, Give Me a Break!

Don't bother looking for any gothic cathedrals built in his honor. You won't find him on any list of saints. In fact, his name sounds like some sort of liver disorder.

As for his place in the Bible, he quickly darts in and out—in the space of just nine verses—to perform only one task. But that task was a big assignment, given to him by the Lord.

Like any of us who are given a stupendous job, Ananias was very uncertain. In fact, he even offered God some background information that just might cause Him to withdraw the assignment.

God knew these details already. He still wanted Ananias to carry through with His request. What was it? Why was it so important? Let's focus on the critical events that led up to this point.

Acts, chapter 9, tells us of the most famous conversion story of all history. The hot-blooded Pharisee, Saul, had just finished seeing Stephen stoned to death. He had even heard this incredible saint ask God to forgive those who were crushing his bones!

Saul asked himself, "How could a bad man die like that?" In seeking to extinguish this nagging question and his tremendous guilt, he plunged into the most violent action possible.

The man from Tarsus bludgeoned believers in Jerusalem. While doing so, he couldn't help but notice that they remained totally serene. What could possibly give them such inner strength?

In a fanatical frenzy he stormed to the Sanhedrin to report that he would hunt down Christians who had escaped to Damascus. The Sanhedrin police force accompanied him during the 140-mile, seven-day journey. Because Saul was a Pharisee, however, he would never lower himself to walk with them. Instead, he walked alone.

But that only made matters worse. Alone, he entered into the sanctuary of his deepest thoughts—especially as he trekked through Christ's home turf of Galilee. What sort of magnetism could Jesus possess, to attract followers with such unbelievable courage?

Then Paul approached Damascus, described by one as "a handful of pearls in a goblet of emerald."[7] As he descended into the beautiful city, suddenly, he was struck blind by a light from heaven. We read about it in Acts 9.

Then a Voice said, "Saul, Saul, why do you persecute me?"

"Who are you, Lord?" Saul asked.

"I am Jesus, whom you are persecuting," He replied. "Now get up and go into the city, and you will be told what you must do."

The blinded Pharisee rose to his feet and was led by the hand into Damascus. There he neither saw, ate, nor drank for three days. He just poured out his heart to God in continual, repentant prayer.

Now he knew the truth and understood the love of Christians for their Saviour. More than anything else, he desired to follow this same Jesus—even if it meant enduring the kind of vicious, unfair persecution he knew of so well.

Still, he asked himself, "Can any Christian forgive me for

---

7. Damascus is one of the oldest cities in the world. Just before reaching Damascus the road climbs Mount Hermon, and down below lies Damascus—a lovely white city in a green plain.

William Barclay: *Daily Study Bible: The Acts of the Apostles* (Philadelphia, Pa.: The Westminster Press, 1953), p. 72.

what I have done? Will any ever accept me as a brother?"

God was already preparing answers to both questions.

In Damascus lived a faithful disciple named Ananias. The Lord said to him, "Go to the house . . . on Straight Street and ask for a man from Tarsus named Saul, for he is praying. In a vision he has seen a man named Ananias come and place his hands on him to restore his sight" (Acts 9:11-12).

Saul's reputation preceded him. Ananias had heard of his violence in Jerusalem and knew of Saul's plans to arrest believers in Damascus. He reiterated these facts to God.

But the answer came back, "Go! This man is my chosen instrument to carry my name before the Gentiles and their kings and before the people of Israel" (v. 15).

Case closed. Ananias went, placed his hands on Saul, and said, *"Brother* Saul, the Lord—Jesus, who appeared to you on the road as you were coming here—has sent me so that you may see again and be filled with the Holy Spirit" (v.18).

Brother Saul. Notice Ananias' words of warm acceptance and complete forgiveness. No little "sermonettes" to induce guilt. No demands for an explanation. No judgments of hidden motives. Not even suspicious looks.

God had supplied the instruction to Ananias—so that now all that was left for him to say was "Brother Saul." Those two words said it all.

One commentator calls Ananias "one of the forgotten heroes of the Christian Church."[8] Ananias heard God's instruction, and promptly acted at a very critical time. And that took courage.

Surely he wondered if his life would be endangered. And why shouldn't a fellow with Saul's track record be completely ostracized? Was it absolutely necessary to follow through with this mission? If so, why couldn't someone else do it—someone more qualified?

These were questions Ananias *never* asked. He didn't need to. God's directive to Him superceded all personal misgivings and doubts.

---

8. Ibid., p. 74.

Julius Caesar once boasted, "I came; I saw; I conquered." Ananias saw, he went, and love conquered. Saul was genuinely welcomed as a brother.

How often we hesitate to say "brother" to believers who have a checkered past. Or who don't have the "right" denominational labels. Or who don't have "enough" years of ecclesiastical seniority. Or who aren't very attractive, say the wrong things, associate with the wrong people, or have no "blue-blood genealogy" in the church. Or . . . .

The warm, forgiving acceptance of Ananias—this courageous "nobody" from Damascus— should put an end to these ways of thinking.

Along with John Wesley we must declare to every man, "If God is your Father, give me your hand, because you're my brother."

Two insignificants with significant courage: Rahab and Ananias. The first dared to defy her king, risk her life, and accept a new people and their God. The second courageously called a hated persecutor "Brother" and offered him warm acceptance, along with his sight.

Two Tips of a Mammoth Iceberg

The two examples that we chose represent scores who, like them, courageously used their "vote" to make a difference.

In the Old Testament, some favorites come to mind:

- *Nathan,* the prophet who rebuked King David for his sin (2 Sam. 12:1-14);
- *Ruth,* who like Rahab, forsook her homeland and journeyed with her mother-in-law (Naomi) to a strange land (Ruth 1:1-11);
- *Caleb,* 85-year-old conqueror, who led Israel's forces into the enemy-infested hill country (Josh. 14:6-13);
- *Mordecai,* Queen Esther's anonymous uncle, who refused to kneel down at the feet of Haman (Es. 1–10).

Likewise, "significant insignificants" surface in the New Testament at critical times to take bold stands. Among them:

- *Joseph,* the simple carpenter who married someone impregnated by the Holy Spirit—in spite of public reaction (Matt. 1:18-21);

- *the widow,* who courageously put her last coins into the temple offering (Mark 12:41-44);
- *Lydia,* who offered her home and hospitality to the homeless Paul in Philippi (Acts 16:13-15);
- *Barnabas,* "the encourager," who affirmed Paul at a time when the disciples were hesitant to accept him (Gal. 2:1-9).

Throughout the annals of history, common people have taken uncommonly courageous stands—in spite of dungeon, fire, or sword.[9]

One martyr declared, "These aren't chains but ornaments. Though my feet are fettered, my soul is still treading the path to heaven. Earth is shut, but heaven is opening. The world recedes, but paradise receives!"[10]

Millions of courageous Christians today declare the sentiments echoed above. They're in East Germany, China, the Soviet Union.

And in our own country, some very courageous stands are being taken daily. Certainly, loss of life is an unlikely threat. But loss of job, marriage, position, wealth, and friendship are ever-present realities.

In fact, hardly a day takes place in every Christian's life that courageous stands are not called for. Subtle temptations to compromise are continual and pervasive. Forces within us seem to cause us to grope for moral shortcuts and pathways of least resistance.

---

9. False charges against early Christians included:
- bringing calamities (e.g., earthquakes), because gods were offended;
- breaking up families—because family deities ceased to be worshiped;
- forsaking old (Jewish) Law;
- treating slaves as brothers (e.g., at Lord's Supper);
- being indifferent to property (i.e., selling goods and pooling resources);
- resorting to violence (e.g., breaking up pagan celebrations);
- being unpatriotic, by not worshiping Caesar;
- becoming atheistic, because they had no material image of their deity (i.e., no visible, tangible evidence)
  (Taken from class notes of Mendel Taylor, at Nazarene Theological Seminary, 1964-1967, in a class called "Heritage of the Christian Church.")
10. Ibid.

We reason: If we were celebrities in the spotlight we would stand taller. If we were blessed with David's kind of internal strength we would "take on giants." If we lived in a nation of intense persecution for our beliefs, then we'd be motivated to boldness. If . . . If . . . If. . . .

The message of this chapter is this: We'll never have ideal conditions that will make Christian courage seem attractive, easy, or convenient. There is always a heavy price to pay—a cost to bear.

But Christ's refreshing presence, and His promise of eternal reward make "standing tall" more than worthwhile. Even (or especially) if we are common, track-mud-on-the-carpet, onions-with-our-hot-dogs, one-vote people.

And here's something else: We're the very kind of folks—not all that different from Rahab and Ananias—whose courage is used by our Heavenly Father to really make a difference. That should give us all a very good feeling and plenty of encouragement.

From People to Principles

It has been jokingly said, "Line up all the philosophers in the world—end to end—and you'll never reach a conclusion!" By contrast, when we line up all the courageous "significant insignificants" in God's Word, we do reach some conclusions.

From these lives, certain biblical principles emerge that are very relevant to us whoever, wherever, and however we are—right now. For they are timeless and totally reliable.

Let's briefly explore biblical teaching on courage, and see how today's Christians measure up.

CHAPTER SIX

God's Eternal Green Light

Even a bad shot is dignified by accepting a duel!

"Courage is a diamond with many facets, and it owes much to setting." (John F. Kennedy)

"Refuse to . . . drift downstream, gathering debris. . . . Press on. Without a quest, life is reduced to wimpy black and white, a diet too bland to get anybody out of bed in the morning." (Charles Swindoll)

I have real problems with two kinds of drivers: *rabbits* and *turtles*. Especially at stoplights.

Someone had rabbits in mind when he sarcastically defined "a millisecond" as "the time from when the light turns until the guy behind you blows his horn."

To have a peddle-to-the-metal speed king run up your back tail pipe is infuriating. You just know that he has a raging case of "type-A personality."

But, to me, there's something even worse: being locked in behind distracted or overly cautious turtles. Drivers who take forever to move when the light turns green. The ones who always seem to be there when it's a short light, or when I'm in a hurry.

The temptation is undeniable. I've wanted to ease up to their bumper and give them a gentle push. Not too hard; just a little visible encouragement. So far, I've resisted.

God must have similar frustrations when He sees how hesitantly we move toward taking courageous stands. There we sit in our prolonged stall.

Like most stoplight intersections in America, God provides us with many "green lights" to see. We've looked at two: the chivalrous, holy example of His Son, and the lives of unsung heroes in His Word.

These, and the many saints who have walked (and walk today) in their footsteps, say to all of us, "Go for it, the light's not getting any greener!"

In addition to these living examples, He provides the "light" of clear, written direction in His Word. This "Drivers Manual" instructs us to be courageous in no uncertain terms.

No Substitutes, Counterfeits, or Facsimiles

When courage is spoken of in the Old Testament, it usually involves a righteous man admonishing God's people to valiantly and confidently enter battle.

For example, Joshua captured five kings (of Jerusalem, Hebron, Jarmuth, Lachish, and Eglon) in a cave. He summoned all men of Israel and said, "Come here and put your feet on the necks of these kings." They did.

Then Joshua declared, "Do not be afraid; do not be discouraged. Be strong and courageous. This is what the Lord will do to all the enemies you are going to fight."

With that, he killed the kings, and hanged them on five trees (Josh. 10:16-26).

By contrast, courage or boldness in the New Testament, has many meanings. Let's explore three:

1. *Courage to speak.* The Greek word, *parrhesiazomai,* means "to speak boldly or wax bold." Acts 19:8 declares: "Paul entered the synagogue and spoke *boldly* there for three months, arguing persuasively about the kingdom of God" (italics added). See also Acts 13:46; 18:26; 26:26; 1 Thessalonians 2:2.

2. *Courage to do.* The Greek word, *tolmao,* refers to boldness in undertaking. To the Corinthian church, Paul says: "I beg you that when I come I may not have to be as *bold* as I expect to be toward some people who think

that we live by the standards of this world" (2 Cor. 10:2, italics added).

3. *Courage to be.* The Greek term, *tharreo,* implies confidence in one's powers—and it refers to a quality of character. We read in Hebrews 13:6, "So we say with *confidence,* 'The Lord is my helper; I will not be afraid. What can man do to me?' "(italics added)[1]

Though it is very helpful to know how courage is used in the Scriptures, we must press on to grasp the underlying teachings about this necessary Christian virtue.

What are its characteristics? How is it attained? What is its price tag? To these and other important matters we now turn our attention.

Straight Ahead

When we examine the flow of biblical material, several important principles related to courage seem to emerge. Furthermore these principles are completely reliable and extremely relevant for us today.

First, our "courage reservoir" builds as we remember how God has brought victory in the past.

The war cry, "Remember the Alamo," motivated Texan soldiers to recall the Lone Star State's proudest moment and to fight with undaunted courage. It was a shot in the arm to the weary fighters.

Likewise, Israel's deliverance from Egypt echoed in the minds of generations and encouraged them to press forward with boldness.

According to the Psalmist, when God's people failed, it was because: "They forgot the God . . . who had done great things in Egypt, miracles in the land of Ham and awesome deeds by the Red Sea" (Ps. 106:21-22).

In all of our lives, we can remember times when our Heavenly Father answered in the nick of time. His answer was

---

1. W.E. Vine, "courage," *An Expository Dictionary of New Testament Words* (Old Tappan, N.J.: Fleming H. Revell Company, 17th edition, 1966), pp. 248-249.

often not just what we expected or requested but He did answer in the way that was best. Our hindsight assures us of this fact.

We do well to savor such memories and to often recall their glorious details. To do so gives us new, or renewed, courage for new battles.

Of course, we must never recall the past to remain there. That would mean a dangerous regression. Rather, our mental "return trip" must always be for the purpose of gaining courage for the future.

Second, our courage supply increases as we affirm God.

The word "affirm" means "to acknowledge worth or to express great confidence in." It's what we do when we cast our ballot on election day. Or when we exchange wedding rings—which someone cynically called "the world's smallest handcuffs." For we baseball fans, it's when we yell for the manager to send our favorite player to the plate as a pinch hitter.

We enjoy being encouraged. Pats on the back feel good. But it's even better when someone truly affirms us. Why? Because that implies the deepest kind of trust and respect.

God dramatically affirmed Jesus on two important occasions.

1. Just before He began His public ministry, at His baptism, God's voice from heaven said: "You are My Son, whom I love; with You I am well pleased" (Mark 1:11).
2. Immediately prior to starting His trip to the cross, He was affirmed on the Mount of Transfiguration. Again came the voice, this time from a cloud overhead, "This is My Son, whom I love. Listen to Him!" (9:7)

Did these affirmations give courage to our Lord? You bet. After the first, He boldly countered Satan's temptations in the wilderness (Matt. 4:1-11).

Following His affirmation on the Mount of Transfiguration, our Lord healed a devil-possessed boy. His disciples wondered why they had been unsuccessful in their attempts.

His reply provided them, and us, with a gold mine of wisdom, "This kind (of demon) can come out only by *prayer*" (Mark 9:29, italics added). To understand His response, let's recap a bit.

Our Heavenly Father affirmed Jesus. Those affirmations made Him incredibly courageous. Why? Because He, in turn, constantly affirmed God in prayer. The formula is this:

$$GA \quad \text{(God's affirmation)}$$
$$+ \underline{AG \quad \text{(Christ's responding affirmation to God through prayer)}}$$
$$= C \quad \text{(courage)}$$

Does this formula work for us? Absolutely. God affirmed us by sending His Son to die for our sins. It was the greatest "I-believe-in-you" message this world has ever known.

Because He lovingly took this initiative we, like Jesus, have the privilege of affirming Him in prayer. And how, exactly, does our prayer affirm Him? Author and friend, Thomas Olbricht, explains in his book *The Power to Be*, "Prayer . . . affirm(s) God, because in prayer we confess our dependence on Him and our powerlessness apart from His power."[2]

When we consistently and fervently pray, we acknowledge His value to our lives. The result? Good things happen. We tap into His generous supply of power. Our confidence level rises. Then it happens: We become bold.

Down deep, we somehow know that there's nothing that we and God can't handle!

Third, the courageous spirit must possess a stalwart faith.

Let's do a flashback to Christ's healing of the demon-possessed lad. The father pleaded: ". . . if you can do anything, take pity on us and help us." " 'If you can'?" said Jesus. *"Everything* is possible for him who believes."

With that assurance, the man exclaimed: "I do believe; help me overcome my unbelief." His son was immediately healed (Mark 9:22-27, italics added).

Once this burdened father reached out in faith, he no longer complained about the disciples' inefficiency, nor looked backward to the details of his child's depressing past.

He experienced a genuine attitude adjustment. Words like

---

2. Thomas H. Olbricht, *The Power to Be: The Lifestyle of Jesus from Mark's Gospel* (Austin, Texas: Sweet Publishing Company, 1979), p. 38.

"expect," "future," "yes," "possible," and "I do" assumed center stage. In short, he assumed a posture of courageous, expectant readiness.

What faith did for him it has done for many. And it will do the same for us. (Let's pause here to refresh ourselves with the words of Hebrews 11.)

What does it mean to have faith? The Bible declares that "faith is being sure of what we hope for and certain of what we do not see" (Heb. 11:1). It's the assurance that comes before the evidence. The smile and "you-just-wait-and-see" look in your eyes.

Faith is the *posture* of courage! The philosopher Cicero declared, "A man of courage is also full of faith."[3]

Somebody formed this helpful acrostic with the letters of "faith":

> **F** (orsaking)
> **A** (ll)
> **I**
> **T** (rust)
> **H** (im).

Forsaking all. Abandoning our artificial securities. Breaking loose from past bitterness and doubt. Putting our full weight on His promises. (See Psalm 37:1-8; Proverbs 3:5-6.)

One more thing. Prayer and faith work together. Jesus said to His disciples, "Have faith in God" (Mark 11:22). But then He continued, "I tell you, whatever you ask for in prayer, believe that you have received it, and it will be yours" (v. 24).

We must pray in faith—even to the point of thanking God for something that has not yet come to pass. That's not fantasy. That's faith! Faith that causes us to arise from our knees with an awesome boldness.[4]

---

3. Lewis Copeland, ed., "courage," *Popular Quotations for All Uses* (Garden City, N.Y.: Garden City Publishing Company, Inc., 1942), p. 93.
4. "Faith is a word with many meanings. It can mean faithfulness (Matt. 24:45). It can mean absolute trust, as shown by some of the people who came to Jesus for healing (Luke 7:2-10). It can mean confident hope (Heb. 11:1). Or, as James points out, it can even mean a barren belief that does not result in

Fourth, courage is often shaped on the fires of trial and persecution.

William Barclay translates Romans 5:3-5 in this way: ". . . let us find a cause of glorying in our troubles; for we know that *trouble* produces *fortitude;* and fortitude produces character; and character produces hope."

The Greek word for "trouble" *(thlipsis)* literally means "pressure." Had a dose of thlipsis lately? Some of us seem to have adopted it as our middle name. Thlipsis of loneliness. Thlipsis of sorrow. Thlipsis of unpopularity. Thlipsis of persecution.

According to Paul, all of that pressure produces "fortitude" *(hupomone)*. The term has, also, been translated "steadfastness" (American Standard Version), "perseverance" (New American Standard Bible) and "endurance" (Goodspeed).

The picture, here, is one of gold that has been tried by fire (1 Peter 1:7). The metal's value is enhanced when the refiner's flames melt away all impurities.

---

good works (James 2:14-26). What does Paul mean when, in Romans, he speaks of saving faith?

"We must be very careful to understand faith as Paul uses the word, because he ties faith so closely to salvation. It is not something we must do in order to earn salvation. If that were true, then faith would be just one more work, and Paul clearly states that human works can never save us (Gal. 2:16). Instead, faith is a gift God gives us because He is saving us (Eph. 2:8). It is God's grace, not our faith, that saves us. In His mercy, however, when He saves us, He gives us faith—a relationship with His Son that helps us become like Him. Through the faith He gives us, He carries us from death into life (John 5:24).

"Even in Old Testament times grace, not works, was the basis for salvation. As Hebrews points out, 'it is not possible for the blood of bulls and goats really to take away sins' (10:4). God intended for His people to look beyond the animal sacrifices to Him, but all too often they instead put their confidence in fulfilling the requirements of the Law, that is—performing the required sacrifices. When Jesus triumphed over death, He canceled the charges against us and opened the way to the Father (Col. 2:12-15). Because He is merciful, He offers us faith. How tragic if we turn faith into a work and try to develop it on our own! We can never come to God through our own faith, any more than His Old Testament people could come through their own sacrifices. Instead, we must accept His gracious offer with thanksgiving and allow Him to plant the seed of faith in us."

From the *Life Application Bible: New Testament,* Bruce B. Barton, ed. (Wheaton, Ill.: Tyndale House Publishers, 1987), p. 385.

Likewise, the highest form of courage emerges from the "fires of adversity." All false and debilitating impurities disappear. Nothing remains but the real thing.

When William Ernest Henley lay in the Edinburgh Infirmary, with one leg amputated and the news that the other must follow, he wrote *Invictus:*

Out of the night that covers me,
Black as the Pit from pole to pole,
I thank whatever gods may be
For my unconquerable soul.[5]

Somehow, he had captured a courage that refused to collapse under the most extreme kind of adversity.

Admittedly, all persecution doesn't produce such a valiant spirit. Just as rainfall makes some ground hard and other soft—depending on the composition of the soil—trial can cause some to become severely embittered, while others are greatly bettered.

If the "soil of the heart" is right, however, trial can enrich the soul and result in increased courage.

In Romans 5, Paul describes the Christian life that is greatly enhanced by pain. But also one whose "courage quotient" has risen dramatically. This person is not likely to be tripped up by minor, daily frustrations—things that disturb those who haven't experienced "the fire."

Saint Peter describes what our attitude should be if we are called on to suffer for our Lord. Listen to his gripping words:

Dear friends, do not be surprised at the painful trial you

---

5. When Beethoven heard about his encroaching deafness, particularly traumatic for a musician, he said, "I will take life by the throat." When Sir Walter Scott became bankrupt because his publishers went broke, he declared, "No man will say 'Poor fellow!' to me; my own right hand will pay the debt!" Another gallant person, undergoing great sorrow, was told, "Sorrow colors your life, doesn't it?" His reply was, "Yes. That it does. But I intend on choosing the colors!" All of these are illustrations of hupomone.
   William Barclay, *The Daily Study Bible: The Letter to the Romans* (Philadelphia, Pa.: The Westminster Press, 1957), p. 70.

are suffering, as though something strange were happening to you. But rejoice that you participate in the sufferings of Christ, so that you may be overjoyed when his glory is revealed . . . if you suffer as a Christian, do not be ashamed, but praise God that you bear that name. (1 Peter 4:12-13, 16)

Fifth, as we act courageously, we must become allergic to the spotlight.

Piety parades are detestable to our Lord. In no uncertain words He declares: "Be careful not to do your 'acts of righteousness' before men, to be seen by them. If you do, you will have no reward from your Father in heaven"(Matt. 6:1).

Courage can easily become an exhibition virtue. Because it is so universally admired, we're tempted to show it off to others—so that others will "eat their hearts out" with envy or treat us with inordinate amounts of respect.

But courage must not become a display. Never. In spite of how much we've had to pray and suffer to attain it. Regardless of what God has helped us to accomplish because of it.

Our courage must be a secret—between us and God. To parade it would be to:
- take credit for something that He gave to us;
- place ourselves in the precarious domain of pride;
- receive our reward on earth rather than in heaven (Matt. 6:3).

Even His enemies realized that Jesus was extremely courageous. One day, they admitted to Him, "Teacher, we know you . . . aren't swayed by men, because you pay no attention to who they are; but you teach the way of God in accordance with the truth" (Mark 12:14).

Jesus didn't even thank them for the compliment. He wasn't about to take a bow and tell them that they were good judges of character. Why? Because He knew they weren't sincere. And even if they had been, His interest wasn't in fame, publicity, or starting a hero cult. Rather, it was exemplifying servanthood to the "poor in spirit." Those who were guaranteed to do zilch for His career!

For many of us, this biblical advice is a pretty big pill to swallow. We compete to attain power, privileges, prestige, and possessions. If we win and gain advantages over others, we're quick to make our victories visible: A "better" selection of friends. Designer products. More expensive vacations.

Courage is a virtue that is not attained easily. It is a rare trophy. A merit of honor. Something that singles us out, makes us seem very distinctive.

But the Bible tells us to keep it hidden. To hide our "courage medal" in the dresser drawer. To destroy our "courage scrapbook." To relinquish all "bragger's rights" to courageous feats we've performed.[6]

Our courage is from Christ, and to Him the credit must return. That is—for now. Someday, if we've been content with incognito courage in this world, we shall receive a reward that is unimaginably glorious.

Paul says so. Quoting Isaiah 64:4 he writes, "No eye has seen, nor ear has heard, no mind has conceived what God has prepared for those who love Him" (1 Cor. 2:9).

This is one prize that's worth waiting for! And keeping a secret!

So, Why the Hesitation?

The Bible speaks of courage in an up-front, clear manner. The principles stated above are repeatedly revealed in stories and doctrinal teachings. To miss them is to ignore them on purpose.

We are all at an intersection with hundreds of green lights and a sea of beckoning fingers, encouraging us to proceed toward the attainment of godly courage. Some of us won't budge. We remain immobilized in a dead stall. Others of us resemble Sunday drivers. We move out very slowly, and

---

6. Another good reason for not boasting about our courage: Our audience may contain people who have been far more courageous than we have. I once heard the story about a man who came through the famous Johnstown (Pennsylvania) Flood. And he told everyone of his heroics. The fellow finally died, met Saint Peter, and immediately requested an audience to relate his well-rehearsed story. Peter declared: "Of course. It will be arranged at once. But there's just one thing you may wish to know: Noah will be in your audience."

poke along—becoming hazardous to ourselves and everyone else.

Both of these miss the meaning of the green light. God has sent a definite message. He expects us to "step on it." To move along. Deliberately. Purposely. And with expectation.

Courage won't "come to us" as we sit and wait. We must, prayerfully and with faith, move toward it—in spite of the risks. Why? Because there is really no other way to be obedient to Him.

So, why do we linger? There are many possible answers, among them:

1. We're overcome by a paralyzing *fear*. John Wesley once said, "Fear freezes and benumbs the soul." That it does. But Paul said, "For God hath not given us the spirit of fear; but of power (i.e., courage), and of love, and of a sound mind" (2 Tim. 1:7, KJV).

2. Our attachment to, or dependence on, some *authority figure* keeps us from venturing forth. Someone spoke the truth when he said, "In the final essence, Jesus is the only one who can control your life without destroying it."

3. Many of us are crippled by a *"sheep complex."* With invisible antennas, we continuously scan to determine what the crowd is thinking. Then we follow along to avoid rejection. Romans admonishes, "Be not conformed to this world" (12:2, KJV).[7]

4. Others of us have an acute case of *"psychic overload."* Like overtaxed computers, we have too many demands on our system. We feel as if we're flooded. Pulled in all

---

7. Sociologist David Riesman has coined the term "other-directed" to describe this sheep-like mentality. He contrasts it with "tradition-directed," which looks to tradition and the past for guidance (e.g., folk cultures), and "inner-directed," which is led by principles implanted in childhood.

Most people conform to the opinions of others or to ways of the past.

A seemingly shrinking minority base their decision-making on personal, internalized convictions.

Jon Johnston, *Will Evangelicalism Survive Its Own Popularity?* (Grand Rapids, Mich.: Zondervan Publishing House, 1980), pp. 105-106.

directions. Unable, or unwilling, to clearly focus on doing what we need to do.[8]

5. More than a few of us depend on *crisis motivation.* We have an inoperable "self-starter." We must be forced by an emergency to be courageous. Otherwise we slump back into lethargy or fantasy.[9]

6. A good number of us are *"shovelers."* Rather than responding with gallant boldness, we say to ourselves, *Let others do it. Why should I get involved?* We shovel our responsibilities onto others.[10]

---

8. Society overloads us with an excessive number of responsibilities. As a result, our concern turns to stress. Why? Because our minds are unable to process the number of demands. T.H. Holmes and R.H. Rahe tell us that our constitution can only take so much overload. Beyond that point, a deterioration of emotional or physical health is likely. Furthermore, our relationships are apt to suffer. This is why persons contracting debilitating illnesses often get divorced, or why parents who lose a child frequently turn on each other. Inordinate quantities of unprocessed overload cause many to search for scapegoats.

See the Holmes-Rahe chart of "life events," and the corresponding amounts of stress that each is likely to cause. In Jon Johnston's *Walls or Bridges: How to Build Relationships That Glorify God* (Grand Rapids, Mich.: Baker Book House, 1988), pp. 237-239.

9. According to my biochemist colleague, recent scientific studies indicate that some people are addicted to their own adrenaline. These individuals have a track record of only being motivated by crisis.

The crisis scares them, which causes their body's defense system to manufacture adrenaline. This, in turn, is their "fuel for motivation." But without the presence of that fuel, they are listless and immobile.

10. Some time ago I saw the following delightful article:

"No turtle objects to mock turtle soup." Recipes for mock turtle soup call for calf's head meat. That suits turtles fine, for they have no wish to be eaten and no sympathy for calves. If I were a turtle, I would be willing to have painted on my back, "Eat Beef."

It's easy to approve sacrifices if the other fellow has to make them. Old men start wars, young men fight them. Rich politicians levy taxes, poor workmen pay them. Church leaders preach sacrifice, hardscrabble pastors make them. It's all mock turtle soup.

Pilate was willing to bend justice and see an innocent man hanged— but he was the judge, not the prisoner. He washed his hands in mock turtle soup.

It's easy to demand heroism from the other fellow. Paul Barnes once told me about a little man who kept saying to a big man, "If I were your size I'd go out there in the jungle and fight lions barehanded."

The big man got tired of having his courage questioned and retort-

7. Many of us have *"spectator-itis."* We're so involved in admiring other courageous persons, that we neglect our own responsibilities. Biblical courage is not meant to be a spectator sport!

8. Finally, scores of us have an acute case of *"heart void."* Because we've never experienced God's Spirit in our beings, we lack necessary inner strength to be courageous.[11]

These appear to be some of the primary reasons why we don't mobilize ourselves in response to God's green lights—why we refuse to experience the joys of courage.

But there is another group of us that is, perhaps, much larger. And it is to this multitude that the remainder of this book is directed.

---

ed, "Look, fellow, there's some little lions out there too." It's easy to order a charge from the safety of the rear lines.

The other day I got a letter from an angry reader blistering me for cowardice. It was unsigned.

In his letter to the Romans, Paul challenges, "You then who teach others, will you not teach yourself?" (2:21, RSV) What if we were all willing to live by the rules we make for others? By the demands we impose on others? By the sacrifices we expect from others? By the heroism we exhort from others? One thing is sure, there would be more turtles simmering in the soup and more calves frisking in the pasture.

William E. McCumber, "McCumber's Maxims" *(Herald of Holiness,* Volume 71, October 15, 1982), p. 17.

11. Wesleyan Arminians refer to a "second work of grace," or "entire sanctification." During the initial born-again experience, specific sins of the past are forgiven. The sinner is pardoned. But in addition, God's Word beckons the believer to a second experience—a time when the Holy Spirit instantaneously cleanses original sin from the heart. A time when the pardoned rebel consecrates his life, and receives purity and power to witness.

It was highly unlikely that Jesus' disciples would remain as unpardoned sinners. Their encounters with Him were too intense. Though immature, they were not rebels. They loved their Master—and sought to learn His ways. They were born again.

But after His death came the Pentecostal experience. A time when "all of them were filled with the Holy Spirit" (Acts 2:4). Result: They were purified, and their newfound courage was amazing. (Compare Peter's boldness in Acts 3, with his denials of Christ prior to the Crucifixion.)

Busy Firemen?

My friend is a fireman in Kansas City. The vast majority of firemen are, no doubt, very courageous like my friend. When flames are leaping out of a twelve-floor apartment house, and trapped people are screaming deliriously, most firemen hurriedly rush inside for the rescue.

But, according to my friend, there are a few who fail to respond in this manner. When lives are at stake, and seconds are of critical importance, they busy themselves with trivial tasks. Like straightening hoses. Checking out ladder joints. Engaging in conversation. Anything and everything except courageously rushing up the ladder to save lives.

No doubt, like most of us, these men are courageous in some areas of their lives. Arguing with their wives. Haggling with their bosses for a raise. Bullying someone while driving on the freeway. Taking a defective product back to the store.

Sure, they're courageous all right—but in areas of small consequence—compared to charging into burning buildings to rescue victims.

One might figuratively put it: many are busy "playing marbles rather than firing cannons"! They are immersed in trifles. Bogged down in making courageous stands on "who cares" issues.

As Christians, we are strongly admonished to be courageous on issues that are near and dear to the heart of God. Issues that are very likely to be ignored by most people—even those who are considered "courageous."

Let's explore these issues in Section Three.

SECTION THREE

COURAGE:
How Can We Best Express It?

CHAPTER SEVEN

Cross My Heart and Hope to Die:
Courage Is Integrity

"Heroes are made every little while, but only one in a million conduct themselves afterwards so that it makes us proud that we honored them at the time." (Will Rogers)

"I believe that every right implies a responsibility, every opportunity an obligation, every possession a duty." (John D. Rockefeller Jr.)

"No wrong choice . . . can persuade God to love you less. Believe this and you will have new courage to make choices, even when you are not sure they [are] the right ones . . ." (Lewis B. Smedes)

A lady once declared, "I don't know what this world is coming to. Someone stole my good Holiday Inn towels right off my clothesline!"

We smile only because we're reminded of our own ethical inconsistencies. The times when our integrity seems to vanish. When we:

- indulge in some dubious "pencil magic" on our income taxes;
- underestimate our vehicular velocity to a traffic judge;
- view X-rated movies while alone in a distant city's hotel;
- give our "afflicted" car a verbal clean bill of health to a prospective buyer;
- become a flirtatious playmate with someone other than our spouse;

- "forget" to turn in a valuable object that we found.

Most of us talk a good game. Lying, cheating, stealing—we say they're repulsive to us. We say we want to be isolated from those who indulge in such moral calamities. Most of us mean what we hear ourselves saying. Our intentions seem pure enough.

Then with about as much warning as an electrical blackout, temptation rears its ugly head. We're faced with making decisions. We must choose between right and wrong or, more difficult yet, between *shades* of right.

All too often our emotions end up winning the tug-of-war with our willpower. We take the way of least resistance: the shortcut. The way that promises to yield the most personal benefit—in spite of who gets hurt or cheated.

A Trio of Conscience Tests

Recently, bags of cash tumbled from an armored truck in Columbus, Ohio. A month or two later, the same thing occurred in San Francisco and Toronto. In all cases, most of the money was grabbed by passersby.[1]

The Ohio episode, in particular, was a unique test of reaction to unexpected riches. A massive traffic jam was created by motorists who stopped to scoop up $2 million worth of bills fluttering in the wind.

Only $100,000 was returned. And many of those who brought back their money received no praise. Mel Kiser, an Ohio Bell repairman who produced $57,000, said: "My mother said she was proud of me—that that's the way she trained me. But my dad said, 'I thought I raised you better than that!' "[2]

---

1. Of the $765,000 lost in San Francisco, approximately $400,000 is missing. California has a felony law against finders-keepers, which applies to amounts above $400.

Ezra Bowen, "What Ever Became of Honest Abe? Maybe He's Home Counting Cash That Fell off a Truck," *Time,* April 4, 1988, p. 68.

2. Phone-in listeners to Columbus radio station WTVN indicated that some 60 percent would have taken the money on the freeway. Concern about a general ethical decline so troubled Columbus Mayor Dana Rinehart that he formed a commission on ethics and values headed by Jeb Stuart Magruder, Watergate ex-con and present minister in the Presbyterian Church (Ibid.).

This strange event is a "mirror" reflecting our nation's commitment to integrity. Study the scenario. Only one-twentieth of the money was returned. Those who stepped forward to relinquish their findings were considered, by many, to be fools.

Many of us are, perhaps, saying to ourselves, "But it's always been that way. Since year one, human beings have been pretty shady characters who do what it takes to gain personal advantage."

In a real sense that's right. Abe Lincoln, who walked miles to return six cents to a customer who overpaid, was an exception, for his time as well as our own.

So why speak of a depletion of integrity in the present?

As author James Dobson says: "Sin is nothing new. Telling lies, welshing on promises, being unfaithful, cheating on taxes, aren't unique to our day. And they surely cannot be laid at the clay feet of an overgeneralized 'social decay.' "

"However," Dobson continues, ". . . through my travels, I do get the overpowering sense that the expression of these evils appears to be increasing. Increasing numbers of well-meaning, but naive, citizens are placing themselves and their families in moral jeopardy."[3]

Take this nation's schools, for instance. In previous eras mischief was tolerated—but not malfeasance; high spirits were accepted—but not low deeds. Today, in urban schools, it is the very brave (and endangered) teacher who reprimands malicious abuse, theft, or lying.[4]

---

3. Ted W. Engstrom, *Integrity,* quote from the foreword by James Dobson (Waco, Texas: Word Books, 1987), pp. ix-x.

4. Marya Mannes, "Dad, What's a Conscience?" *Newsweek,* April 15, 1974, p. 11.

Author Dale Evans Rogers presents the following results of a survey of 2,000 high school seniors in California:

- 75 percent admit to copying another's exam (most did it repeatedly).
- 73 percent owned up to using crib notes to cheat on exams.
- 51 percent confessed to copying, word for word, from books—and presenting it as their own ideas.
- 97 percent say they have witnessed others cheating on exams.
- 42 percent claim there are some "very good reasons for cheating" like making high grades for college entrance and an eventual high-paying career.

Consider the professional world. We hear sordid accounts of sports stars involved in sexual affairs, financiers attempting "cloak-and-dagger" deals, social scientists reporting spurious findings, politicians receiving "slush funds" from corporations, and televangelists enmeshed in all of the above—and more. Today almost every job seems to have an undertow of powerful temptations that pulls us away from integrity.

And along with these, we have plenty of tailor-made rationalizations to "whitewash" our questionable deeds. We've all heard (or used) them: "I'm only doing what's necessary to survive." "In this day it's expected." "My actions won't really hurt anybody." "I'm doing it for my wife and children." "It's my only way of getting back at the system."

Because our societal fabric isn't woven with strong, ethical fibers, those of us with integrity must have a lion's share of moral courage.

To be such a person is commendable indeed. Alexander Pope put it well: "An honest man is the noblest work of God."

But to understand what is involved in becoming such a stalwart, let's explore some dimensions contained in this appealing quality that we call "integrity."

There's more here than meets the eye.

And it's of great relevance in the family room as well as the classroom—the boardroom as well as the bedroom.

Comprehending the "I" Word

Put very simply, *integrity* comes from the word *integer,* which implies being *whole, indivisible,* and *singular.* In short, it is a single-hearted mind-set.[5]

Integrity is being true-blue, rock-ribbed, straight-shooting, credible, on the level, non-fictitious.

When we have integrity, there is an internal-external consis-

---

● Only 1 percent declare they would report on a friend whom they saw cheating. David O. Savage, "High School Test Cheating: 75 Percent Admitted Cite Pressure," *L.A. Times,* April 7, 1986, Part 1, page 3; Summarized in Dale Evans Rogers' *Only One Star: A Cure for the Celebrity Syndrome* (Dallas: Word Publishing, 1988), p. 128.

5. Engstrom, op. cit., taken from summary on front book jacket.

tency. What we say, we mean. What we seem to be, we are. What we "talk," we "walk."

But that's the ideal. Most of us appear to be somewhat downrange on the integrity continuum.

Dr. Lawrence Kohlberg, a Harvard psychologist, has pinpointed six plateaus of moral development. Let's venture a guess as to where we're located.

Stage one: obedience and punishment. Right is what authorities command. The underlying motive is fear of punishment, not respect for authority or values.

Stage two: back-scratching. When people begin to seek a return for their favors. It's the "I'll-do-for-you-but-only-if-you-reciprocate" mentality. Kohlberg terms it "the morality of the marketplace."

Stage three: conformity. Good behavior is that which pleases or helps others, and is approved by them. The evaluations and expectations of peers are particularly strong.

Stage four: law-and-order. What is right is doing one's duty, showing respect for authority and maintaining the given social order. What the law commands transcends all other considerations.

Stage five: social contract. Right is defined in terms of the general rights of individuals, as agreed upon by the whole society (e.g., U.S. Constitution).

Stage six: universal principles. Morality is based on decisions of conscience made in accordance with self-chosen principles of "right"—principles which are universal and consistent.[6]

6. Like Swiss child psychologist Jean Piaget, Kohlberg believes that the ability

According to the psychologist, most of us never rise above stage four. We're obsessed with our own rights under the law. We're not really concerned about how our actions impact the rights of others (stage five). Nor can we even relate with those—like Gandhi, Socrates, Mother Teresa—who followed their consciences, regardless of the cost (stage six).

To the Victor Goes the Reward!

Though rare to find in its purest form, and though it demands great courage, integrity is worthy of our pursuit.

For one thing, it does wonders for ourselves. Realizing this fact, Edgar Guest offers this thought-provoking poem:

Myself

I have to live with myself, and so
I want to be fit for myself to know,
I want to be able, as days go by,
Always to look myself straight in the eye;
I don't want to stand, with the setting sun,
And hate myself for the things I've done.

I don't want to keep on a closet shelf
A lot of secrets about myself,

---

to reason about moral problems develops by stages. Morally, a child must "crawl" before he can "walk." Kohlberg's basic premise is that moral development, like intellectual development, is a natural process that teachers can nurture in children.

Furthermore, these stages are based on the maturation of the mind. Stage one is typical of children up to age seven. Stage two is found in preadolescents. Stage three is characteristic of adolescents. Stage four is the stage in which most people remain.

He asserts that each stage in moral reasoning is psychologically and philosophically more mature than the previous stage. Thus, the first two stages he terms "preconventional morality," because they are dominated by the child's egocentric needs and desires. The second two are labeled "conventional morality," because they are based on a recognition of the rules laid down by society. Finally, the last two stages are termed "postconventional morality," because they are rooted in principles of justice by which the individual judges himself, other people, and society.

Kenneth L. Woodward, "Moral Education," *Newsweek,* March 1, 1976, p. 74.

And fool myself, as I come and go,
Into thinking that nobody else will know
The kind of a man I really am;
I don't want to dress up myself in sham.

I want to go out with my head erect,
I want to deserve all men's respect;
But here in the struggle for fame and pelf
I want to be able to like myself.
I don't want to look at myself and know
That I'm bluster and bluff and empty show.

I can never hide myself from me;
I see what others may never see;
I know what others may never know,
I never can fool myself, and so,
Whatever happens, I want to be
Self-respecting and conscience free.[7]

Again, a primary benefactor of our integrity is ourselves. This is true not only of life, but also of memories that linger beyond our mortal existence.

Respected minister, Charles H. Spurgeon, once wrote: "A good character is the best tombstone. Those who loved you, and were helped by you, will remember you when forget-me-nots are withered. Carve your name on hearts, and not on marble."[8]

That's integrity, a better long-term investment than the best Certificate of Deposit known to man!

In addition to ourselves, our integrity has a wholesome ripple effect on those around us. With every act of honesty, and expression of authentic credibility, people feel affirmed and encouraged about mankind.

Furthermore, the level of trust begins to rise—replacing the rampant looking-out-for-number-one mentality of our day.

---

7. Hazel Felleman, *Best Loved Poems,* "Myself," by Edgar A. Guest, p. 91.
8. Engstrom, op. cit., p. 67.

Muscles relax. Smiles appear. Anxiety lessens.

Ted Engstrom, in his book entitled *Integrity,* speaks a truth: "When we can no longer depend on one another or do what we said we would do, the future becomes an undefined nightmare."[9]

In our day of specialization and automation, it is imperative that we possess a mutual trust. Our doctors must be trusted when they operate on our hearts. Our pilots must be trusted when they're landing their 747s. Our bankers must be trusted with our life savings. Our ministers must be trusted when they "rightly divide the word of truth."

Once again, with every deed of integrity comes an elevation in the level of trust. Result: our world is made a better place. One in which people can be reconciled to one another in peace and in love.

Third, in addition to ourselves and others, the One above considers our integrity as an important form of worship. We honor Him and reflect His very nature when we're morally upright.

That's why His Word has so much to say about integrity.[10]

It Jumps Out at Us

The Bible is replete with appeals for integrity. Even the slowest of learners is able to grasp the importance our Heavenly Father attributes to this virtue. After Solomon completed the temple and royal palace, God said to him, "As for you, if you walk before Me in *integrity* of heart and uprightness . . . I will

---

9. Ibid., p. 2.

10. The Bible refers directly to *integrity* sixteen times. In Hebrew, *"thom"* means *whole* and *complete,* and is translated *integrity.* The plural, *"thummim"* suggests a ceremonial ornament which was only worn by the high priest. At times, high-level decisions could only be made by consulting the *"Urim* and *Thummim"* (Ezra 2:63).

Evidently, these were stone objects, gemstones representing the twelve tribes of Israel, or a gold plate. Significance: This object suggests that "integrities" (plural of *thom*) were required to stand before God and learn of His will. Ephesians 6:14 refers to the "breastplate of righteousness," which is a kind of spiritual *thummim* that Christians should wear. (Ibid., p. 12, "Urim," taken from *Unger's Bible Dictionary* (Chicago: Moody Press, 1966), pp. 1128-29.

establish your royal throne over Israel forever" (1 Kings 9:4-5).

The psalmist declares, "Judge me, O Lord, according to my righteousness, according to my *integrity*, O Most High" (7:8). Again, he says, "May *integrity* and uprightness protect me, because my hope is in you" (25:21). Then he testifies, "In my *integrity* you uphold me and set me in your presence forever" (41:12).

In Proverbs, we're told that God "holds victory in store for the *upright*, He is a shield to those whose walk is blameless" (2:7). In Bible times people wore long robes. If one stooped, there was room for stolen goods or weapons. Standing upright literally meant, "I've got nothing to hide."

How about this proverb? "The *integrity* of the upright guides them, but the unfaithful are destroyed by their duplicity" (11:3). Sooner or later there is a day of reckoning. As Lincoln said: "You can fool some of the people some of the time, but not all of the people all of the time."

These admonitions are extremely helpful, but virtue is best found in a life. And perhaps few ever lived with more integrity than Job.

The Bible describes him as *blameless* and *upright* (Job 1:1). Does that mean he was patient, in the sense of being uncomplaining? Not exactly. It seems as though only David out-complained Job.

Then, how was his integrity manifested?

1. *He had a right relationship with God.* We are told that he "feared God and shunned evil" (1:1).
2. *He lived a righteous life in his community.* Once again, he was thought of as "blameless and upright."
3. *He was characterized by faithfulness and steadfastness.* In the midst of incomprehensible physical and mental torture he declared: "Though He slay me, yet will I hope in Him"(Job 13:15). "I know that my Redeemer lives"(Job 19:25).[11]

---

11. This outline was taken from an October 1988 chapel address, given by President Homer J. Adams, Trevecca Nazarene College, Nashville, Tenn.

Jesus describes Nathanael as a person "in whom there is nothing false" (John 1:47). Are there any of us who wouldn't give everything we own to hear our Lord say that about us?

And how about Christ's integrity? He always spoke the unvarnished truth. And in direct, simple words. That's why He forbade oath-taking and said, "Simply let your 'Yes' be 'Yes,' and your 'No,' 'No' " (Matt. 5:33-37). As believers, our word must *be* our oath.

We live in a world where style seems more important than substance. Where oaths are required in courts, so people will feel coerced to tell the truth. Where speakers operate under the motto: "If you can't dazzle 'em with brilliance, baffle 'em with confusion."

Jesus manifested integrity in so many other ways. He called the leaders in Jerusalem liars, blind men, fools, serpents, vipers. He refused to display a fake humility by concealing his extraordinary knowledge. He warned people that they were moving toward perdition and painted their ruin in words which causes the human heart to shudder.

Since His earthly existence, many uncomplimentary things have been said about our Lord. But even His harshest critics have hesitated to call Him an intentional deceiver. They've said He was mistaken, called Him a visionary, fanatic, and dreamer—but not a person capable of telling a lie. As Charles Edward Jefferson so aptly put it: "There is something so pure and frank and noble about Him that to doubt His sincerity would be like doubting the brightness of the sun."[12]

So the evidence is overwhelming. There is a thread of integrity that connects the earliest biblical patriarchs with the life of our sinless Saviour, with Christians who have lived since then until our present day. The words and tempo of this great "biblical hymn" may vary throughout time, but the song is essentially the same!

Unfortunately, not all who claim to live by biblical principles, are singing this "song." Or, if they are, they're singing off-key. And that should concern all of us, just as it concerns our Lord.

---

12. Charles Edward Jefferson, *The Character of Jesus* (New York: Grosset and Dunlap, 1907), pp. 63-64.

You Call It!

Question: Do you have Christian friends who seem a little flaky when it comes to being up-front and honest? Persons who do or say things that you really wonder about?

Something really bothers me, and I might as well confess it. I continuously observe those who claim no allegiance to biblical teaching—but who manifest impeccable integrity. On the other hand, I'm perplexed by ethical practices of some who profess to be ardent followers of Jesus.

I know what you're saying to yourself, *Yes, but sinners are ethically upright for the wrong reasons. Morality is their "religion" or their crutch.* No doubt there's truth to your response. But does that let the suspect Christians off the hook?

Allow me to share three brief illustrations, which will give a better idea of what I'm getting at.

Illustration number one. There's this couple I know who are both leaders in their church. They're faithful in attendance, give a tithe, know hymns by heart, close their eyes while praying. In general they're thought to be A-OK laymen.

In all ways they're pretty typical. Sure, like all of us, they have their idiosyncrasies. The lady is known to be fairly close with money. She spends plenty of time at flea markets and garage sales. And—can you believe this—she requires that her children use no more than two squares of toilet tissue per wipe! Oh well. I guess we all have our quirks.

But this couple frequently takes their family on weekend jaunts in their camper. And when they do, they think nothing of pulling up to a Holiday Inn, sneaking in the swimming pool gate, and taking a dip that lasts for several hours.

Notice that I said they "sneak," which implies knowledge of wrongdoing. And when inside, they're confronted with signs declaring: THIS POOL IS RESTRICTED TO PATRONS STAYING IN OUR HOTEL.

Now, in describing these experiences to us, this couple seems to pass off their actions as clever, innocent fun.

I just wonder if their children sneak into the hotel bathrooms to experience the pleasure of having sufficient quantities of toilet paper!

Illustration number two. Like most of you, I hold ministers in the highest regard. There is something very special about these who reach people with the Gospel. But the other day a minister approached my wife and me, as we were having a cup of tea at an evangelism conference. This very prominent clergyman brought up the issue of hotel rates. Knowing that we travel a great deal, he proceeded to brag about his gimmick.

In order to stay at the best places, at a fraction of the regular cost, this guy had cards printed that gave the impression that he was a bona fide travel agent. And the front desk personnel never questioned his claim. As a result his church was saved a nice chunk of money.

The second ingenious idea was requested of my wife, who is a travel consultant. A minister asked her to do two airline tickets. But his request included something that didn't seem quite cricket.

He realized that staying over Saturday night cuts most fares in half. He also knew that neither of his trips included a layover.

A clever thought occurred to him: Why not simply put the two halves together? Then it would appear as though the Saturday night requirement had been satisfied on both trips.

Well, he spilled out his scheme to my wife, who suffers from an overactive conscience. Though uncomfortable about the idea, she went ahead and checked it out with her boss. Sure enough, she was told that, if the airlines caught wind of the minister's plan, he could be in serious difficulty.

It was embarrassing, but she had to do it. The minister was phoned, and he was kindly told that his request could not be granted. His comment: "But I hear of other ministers doing it all the time." Whoops!

Illustration number three. Those of us who have spent time on a college campus realize how important it is for faculty members to earn their doctoral degree. Without one, they're made to feel about as welcome as a cat at a mouse convention.

At one Christian college I know of, a certain doctor-less professor decided that he could take no more psychological abuse. He had endured insults and lower salary for fifteen years and that was long enough. It was high time for him to receive acceptance!

He traveled to a distant city and enrolled in a "degree mill" program. After paying a handsome amount, filling out a few papers, and taking a few superficial courses, he was granted his "Mickey Mouse" diploma.

The next week, he slapped the impressive certificate on the desk of his dean, and proudly declared himself an authentic doctor. It was promptly announced, and congratulations poured in. Not incidently, he received the long-awaited, substantial raise in salary.

Then it happened. It was either a one-in-a-million happenstance or, more likely, the providence of God. The chairman of his discipline somehow ran into an official from the counterfeit school. As they conversed, he was aghast as the latter described its laughable requirements.

It was a toss-up between the difficulty of getting a doctorate from that school and passing the "Pepsi test"—or the qualifying exam for a Disneyland driver's license. Finally, the "beans were spilled," as the make-believe administrator revealed the identity of the mutually-recognized professor.

The chairman was stunned. How could his trusted faculty member attempt such a ridiculous stunt? He must be out of his mind!

You can anticipate the remainder of the story. The professor was confronted, then promptly and unceremoniously fired. Furthermore, his college reviewed the painful lesson they had learned.

I've always wondered if the guy sent back his diploma and requested a refund. Or here's a better idea: Maybe he should have been made to return tuition money to his students!

Let's pause long enough to recap the reasons given in the preceding illustrations:

Illustration number one—*having innocent fun.*

Illustration number two—*saving the church money; and, other ministers are doing it.*

Illustration number three—*achieving acceptance and respectability.*

Well, what's your verdict? Are these legitimate and acceptable? Perhaps we are in danger of taking this "integrity business" too far? Maybe we should not insist on high ethical standards that seem, to so many, to be unreasonable and even unattainable?

My Ongoing Battle

I must confess my own difficulty in meeting the rigorous standard of integrity. "Convenience" deceptions are a continual temptation—especially:

- when the unvarnished, bold truth appears to be too much for some to handle (e.g., persons who are emotionally explosive, terminally ill, or new to the faith);
- when it's a matter of giving someone credit for a thought he originated, but I expounded on, in my writing; (Sure, I end up doing it but sometimes quite begrudgingly.)
- when my loophole-conscious tax man encourages me to be excessively generous in estimating certain expenses;
- when a student with a mediocre academic record but a winsome personality, requests me to write a positive letter of recommendation;
- when the concord grapes look so delicious and tasty in our local supermarket.

Then there's money. My problem seems to arise when I feel that I'm being unfairly assessed—as in the time we bought our first house. Getting enough for a down payment required a complete exhaustion of our meager monetary supply. To put it bluntly, we were broke. Busted.

In determining the amount of loan we needed, all escrow fees were figured in. It appeared to be a neat package.

Well, a year later the telephone rang. It was the escrow company. They had discovered a miscalculation on their part. I owed them $1,000.

Have you ever had a rush of twelve different emotions at once? Then you know how I felt. But the predominant feeling corresponded to my basic thought, namely, that I didn't owe them a dime!

It was their mistake. They admitted it. No court could possibly stick me with some dated fee that an escrow company retrieved from "left field." I would ignore the call and the whole matter. Period.

Unfortunately, it wasn't really a period. It was more like a comma. My conscience tape began to roll on its own. And its "off button" wouldn't work—no matter how hard I pushed it.

I said to myself, "I'll put this whole thing to rest by getting confirmation from my friends." They heard my explanation and, predictably, sided with my decision. That's it. Time to close the file drawer.

But the file drawer wouldn't stay closed. And I was driven to ask myself the only question that really matters: *"Do I owe the money?"*

I felt certain that, a quick review of the figures, would demonstrate their error. So I retrieved the sheets, and used my calculator. Then came the bottom line reality: I did, in fact, owe the money. They had made an honest mistake.

With that, I telephoned the company and asked to speak to the president. He listened intently as I explained my situation. I hoped that my sincerity would cause him to excuse the whole matter.

His response: "Sorry about our mistake, but you really do owe the money."

Now why did he have to use *that* choice of words. It only added to my discomfort.

Then it was that I realized that God had me cornered. I simply had to pay the money—money we really didn't have.

As my conversation with the president continued, I detected a note of compassion in his voice. After telling him that I was a Christian who wanted to do the right thing, his position softened. Result: He agreed that a $500 payment would be sufficient.

The money was sent. The tape recorder of my conscience stopped playing. The file drawer closed. And, down deep, I felt good.

Should I have returned the money? Was I obeying a biblical principal, or simply being driven by an overly sensitive, misdirected conscience? You be the judge.

But regardless of your verdict, we can agree on one thing: biblical integrity *is* essential. Plain and simple—for our inner peace and for our Christian witness.

And because our world manifests such an extreme shortage of this crucial spiritual quality, perhaps it's quite permissible for us to go a little overboard in demonstrating it.

CHAPTER EIGHT

Your Heartbreak in Me:
Courage Is Compassion

"Conservative : someone who throws a 25-foot rope to a drowning man 50-feet away and says, 'Swim for it; it'll build character.' Liberal: a person who throws a 50-foot rope to a drowning man 25-feet away, then walks away to do 'another good deed.' "

"Must one point out that from ancient times a decline in courage has been considered the beginning of the end?" (Aleksandr Solzhenitsyn)

"Granted, if we go His way we will be broken, but if we don't, we will be crushed." (Mel Rich)

To understand compassion, it is helpful to examine its opposite—cruelty.

There are songs about cruel people. One tells about "hard-hearted Hannah, gal of Savannah, [who] poured water on a drowning man." Another portrays the story of "Leroy Brown—meaner than a junkyard dog."

Certain occupations are reputed to attract persons with ice water in their veins.

I heard about a lawyer whose yacht sank in a pool of sharks. As he swam for safety, the man-eaters immediately parted to let him through. They considered it a professional courtesy!

And there's a story about a man who prepared to have a heart transplant. His doctors asked him to choose between two available hearts: one from a young athlete; the other from a middle-aged college dean. To their surprise, he promptly chose the dean's, saying, "It'll last me much longer, because it probably hasn't ever been used."

Speaking of the heartless, perhaps there are few who are considered more calloused than win-driven, high school football coaches.

One afternoon, during a brutal scrimmage in 90-degree heat, my quarterback friend was "flattened" by a red-dogging linebacker—who nailed him from his blind side. There he lay on the turf, racked with intense pain. His "compassionate" coach walked over to where he was lying, looked at him, and snarled, "Don't mash my grass!"

Even a cursory look at history reveals a plethora of monstrous rulers. Rulers who concurred with a principle put down by sixteenth-century philosopher, Niccolo Machiavelli, namely: "It is better for leaders to be feared than to be loved."

One such person was King Herod (47 B.C.–4 B.C.), who constructed Jerusalem's temple. He was a generous man, having melted down his own gold dinner plate to buy corn for starving countrymen. But he was insane with suspicion. Anyone suspected as a rival was permanently eliminated.

We all know that Herod attempted to kill baby Jesus—by annihilating all of Bethlehem's male infants (Matt. 2:7-18).

He murdered his wife, Mariamne, and dipped her in honey. (I told you he was insane!) Also he assassinated his mother-in-law, Alexandra, and his oldest son, Antipater. Not wanting to show favoritism, he wiped out his other two sons, Alexander and Aristobulus.

Herod's savage, warped nature is vividly seen in his arrangements for his own death. Told that his seventy-year-old body was being eaten by worms, he went to his spacious Jericho palace to die. Immediately, he gave orders to arrest Jerusalem's most distinguished citizens on trumped-up charges.

Then, he instructed that these people must be slaughtered the moment he died. Why? His sick mind reasoned that nobody would ever mourn for him. But if these people were butchered on the day of his death, that would guarantee sympathy throughout the land.[1]

Herod was cruel, as were scores of other leaders throughout the history of mankind.[2] But what does this barbarism have to do with us?

Offensive Unit on the Field!

Today, we hear about a continuous flow of crime in our cities. And of people's tempers getting out of hand, at places like sports events.

But most of us do not react so harshly and irresponsibly. We are basically decent persons who find it difficult to kill a June bug, or to turn down a Girl Scout peddling her cookies.

---

1. William Barclay, *Daily Study Bible Series: The Gospel of Matthew* (Philadelphia, Pa.: The Westminster Press, 1956), pp. 19-20.

As leaders, Herod and Jesus have been contrasted in these ways:

Herod	*Jesus*
selfish	compassionate
murderer	healer
immoral	just and good
political opportunist	servant
king over small territory	king over all creation

From the *Life Application Bible: New Testament,* Bruce B. Barton, ed. (Wheaton, Ill.: Tyndale House Publishers, Inc., 1987), p. 106.

2. The king of ancient Assyria, Ashurbanipal (669 B.C.), was known for his ruthlessness. For example, when he conquered and destroyed the Egyptian city of Thebes (No-Amon), in 663, he was merciless to his captives. They were maimed, skinned alive, and even boiled in oil.

"These atrocities are particularly disappointing in view of the fact that, only 125 years before, the Assyrians had responded penitently to the preaching of Jonah."

From *The Narrative Bible,* narrated by F. LaGard Smith (Eugene, Ore.: Harvest House Publishers, 1984), p. 929.

One of the cruelest rulers of all time was a Pasha, named Ahmad (1805-1775 B.C.), who his own people termed "Jazzar" (the cut-throat). He is said to have had a Jewish adviser, Haim Farhi, in his stronghold at Akko (biblical Acre; Greek/Roman Ptolemais). Ahmad imposed this agreement on Farhi: Anytime you give me bad advice, you shall die.

Each time you give me advice that brings me good luck, you shall have one member of your body cut off. Legend has it that the adviser survived many years, but without arms, legs, ears, nose, etc.

Zev Vilnay, *Israel Guide* (Jerusalem, n.p., 1984), pp. 396-402.

In our own era, we are reminded of such leaders as Adolph Hitler, Pol Pot, the Khmer Rouge (Cambodia), and Idi Amin (Uganda). History books "drip blood from the cruelty of world leaders, attesting to man's inhumanity to man."

Commendable? Perhaps. But Jesus demands more, much more. His Word calls on us to take the initiative for right. Not only to refrain from being cruel, but to lovingly reach out to those who have been victimized.

We are to act this way even when it seems foolish. And we must reach out in love even when it is inconvenient—which is most of the time. These actions require a kind of courage that many of us naturally shy away from.

But sometimes we see glimpses of such chivalry, and when we do, it refreshes and inspires us.

There's the New York family that combines their efforts to make and distribute hundreds of sandwiches for the homeless. They received well-deserved acclaim on television's "Sixty Minutes."

Then, I must tell you about a "freeway Good Samaritan" I just heard about. One of the nicest and most talented persons I know had a traumatic blowout on her way to our church—where she serves as worship leader.

Cars whizzed by at their customary breakneck speeds. Many "rubbernecked" but none stopped. That is . . . until a certain man pulled up. With a big smile, he got out of his car and offered to help.

He inconvenienced himself that morning. He helped change the tire even though considerable time was required, and the grease took its toll on his clothes.

Upon his completion of the task, my friend thanked him profusely. His reaction: "I am the one who receives the blessing."

As he drove off, my relieved friend couldn't help but notice his license plate. It read: LVG 2B KD (living to be kind).

So the point has been established that compassion must be seen as an offensive, rather than simply a defensive strategy. It charges rather than barricades. As one writer states it, compassion must be "dressed up in work clothes and sent out onto the streets [and freeways] of men."

But before we can be truly compassionate, it is imperative that we comprehend what it is. Let's lean forward to have a closer look.

Reaching Out to Touch

One dictionary defines *compassion* as "love's emotional response to actual distress, or some impending calamity, in the life of another."[3]

The term is derived from the Latin words "pati" and "cum," which together mean "to suffer with." Thus, to be compassionate means to enter the arena of pain, to share in brokenness and anguish, to cry out with those in misery.[4]

In the New Testament, the Greek word most commonly used is *splangknon*, which suggests feeling great pity, close identification with, and intense feeling. Its literal meaning is "being moved in one's innermost being."[5]

God's compassion results from the infinite greatness of His love. Seeing the misery of creation, the Creator . . . conspicuously displayed His empathy in the gift of His Son (John 3:16).

And Jesus is our Heavenly Father's embodiment of compassion. He felt it toward the widow, as her only son's draped casket passed by. He felt it toward the "harassed and helpless crowds" who followed Him "like sheep without a shepherd" (Matt. 9:36;14:14). He felt it toward the 4,000 who had not eaten for three days (Mark 8:2), and toward two blind men sitting beside the Jericho Road (Matt. 20:34).

His response, in each of these situations, was never forced. It flowed naturally from a heart that was perfectly attuned to His Father's will. Nor was it paternalistic—to satisfy a need to control, overpower, or impress. Finally, it was in no sense manipulative. Those He helped "owed" Him nothing. In gratitude and faith, many responded to His teachings afterward, but they made those decisions themselves. He exercised no semblance of mind control.

Jesus gave no-strings-attached, free, loving compassion.

3. W. Stephen Gunter, "compassion," *Beacon Dictionary of Theology*, Richard S. Taylor, ed. (Kansas City, Mo.: Beacon Hill Press), 1983, 127.
4. Donald P. McNeill, Douglas A. Morrison, Henri J.M. Nouwen, *Compassion: A Reflection on the Christian Life* (Garden City, N.Y.: Image Books, 1966), p. 6.
5. W.E. Vine, *An Expository Dictionary of New Testament Words* (Old Tappan, N.J.: Fleming H. Revell Company, 1966), p. 218.

And it was straight from the deepest recesses of His sinless, God-aligned heart. That required courage.

Furthermore, His life and teachings broadcast a message to us loud and clear: The Christian way is, in reality, the way of compassion. To His disciples He declares, "Be merciful (compassionate) just as your Father is merciful" (Luke 6:36).[6]

This theme is vividly underscored in the Parable of the Prodigal Son. Capture the beautiful picture of this dramatic homecoming: "But while he was a long way off, his father saw him and was filled with compassion for him; he ran to his son, threw his arms around him and kissed him" (Luke 15:20).

John speaks of our need for compassion when he states, "If anyone sees his brother in need but has no pity on him, how can the love of God be in him? Dear children, let us not love with words or tongue but with actions and in truth" (1 John 3:17-18).

In university language, John is telling us that compassion is not an elective. It is a required course—absolutely necessary for graduating into heaven.

The first-century church learned its lessons well. Here is how it was described by Aristides, an ancient philosopher:

Falsehood is not found among them; and they love one another, and from widows they do not turn away their esteem; and they deliver the orphan from him who treats him harshly. And he who has gives to him who has not, without boasting. And when they see a stranger, they take him into their homes and rejoice over him as a very brother; for they do not call them brethren after the flesh, but brethren after the spirit and in God. And when-

---

6. Former Vice President, Hubert Humphrey, had a unique way of expressing himself. Speaking to a group of Christian men, he held up a long pencil and said, "Gentlemen, just as the eraser is only a very small part, and is only used when a mistake is made, so compassion is only called upon when things get out of hand." His conclusion: "The main part of life is competition; only the eraser is compassion."

But that was Hubert Humphrey talking. Our biblical blueprint considers compassion to be much more than an eraser. It's that too, all right, but much more (McNeill, op. cit.).

ever one of their poor passes from the world, each one of them according to his ability gives heed to him and carefully sees to his burial. And if they hear that one of their number is imprisoned or afflicted on account of the name of their Messiah, all of them anxiously minister to his necessity, and if it is possible to redeem him they set him free.

And if there is among them any that is poor and needs, and if they have no spare food, they fast two or three days in order to supply the needy their lack of food.[7]

This is inspiring to contemplate, but the question remains: What evidences of compassion are we observing in the lives of our Christian brothers and sisters today?

Surprisingly, this New Testament virtue can pop up in some pretty unlikely people.

Meet a "Porcupine Care-bear"

My wife has this compassionate friend. Now, if you were around her for ten minutes, you'd probably conclude that she is anything but compassionate.

This gal exudes abrasiveness. Positive attitude? Norman Vincent Peale would probably turn from her and run. Winsomeness? Not really. Her entire demeanor betrays her.

You get the picture. My wife's friend is considered, by many, to be one super turn-off. That's why she is rarely invited to anyone's home.

And that's why my wife volleys snide comments when she is seen relating to her: "Why do you even bother talking to her?" "You mean you're actually friends?"

Does the lady pick up these rejection cues? You bet. Down deep, she realizes that she has about as much chance being accepted as Charles Manson has becoming the Chief Justice of the Supreme Court.

And this really hurts her. As a result she is abrasive to

7. Robert E. Webber, *The Secular Saint* (Grand Rapids, Mich.: Zondervan Publishing House, 1979), p. 84.

conceal her intense pain. Sure, it is a survival technique. But it is, also, a crying-out for attention. In effect, she is saying: "Please recognize that I exist." "I count for something, don't I?"

But, don't close the book on her yet. Cease categorizing. Otherwise, you'll be mistaken.

My perceptive spouse has always seen this lady for what she is, one overactive "compassion dispenser." She gives from the heart—in a way in which people aren't made to feel obligated. And she does so continuously, without fanfare. Incognito.

Here are just some of her "acts of compassion." She:

- sits with sick hospital patients who have had surgery;
- continually writes notes of encouragement;
- arranges large dinner parties in her home for the needy and elderly;
- calls whenever she senses that there might be an impending crisis; (e.g., Southern California forest fire, earthquake, flood).

Now, most people don't wish to get close enough to learn of her compassionate gestures. When they see her coming, one word flashes across their mental screen: *avoidance!*

Some have noticed her acts of compassion, but quickly discount them. In their opinion she cancels out any good works by being so hard to get along with. Such persons haven't bothered to examine the underlying reasons for her behavior—nor tried to relate to her world.

Lately, I've given considerable thought to this entire scenario. It seems that there are some valuable lessons to learn:

1. The lady's compassion is to be applauded. Nevertheless, it must be admitted that she undercuts its impact by continuing to behave offensively. How many of us fall into this same trap?

As stated in *Walls or Bridges: How to Build Relationships That Glorify God,* we often inadvertently turn off others by being oblivious, obnoxious, or ostentatious.[8]

---

8. Jon Johnston, *Walls or Bridges: How to Build Relationships That Glorify God* (Grand Rapids, Mich.: Baker Book House, 1988), p. 75.

We fail to remember that others often judge us by the visible manifestations of our personality. And when our observers are non-Christians, this judgment is frequently extended to other Christians—and even to the Lord we serve.

It behooves us to sandpaper, file, and buff the rough edges of our personalities. And to forever reject the notion that "we are what we are, and can never change."

2. *The elitist responses of her accusers do not seem to "cut New Testament pie." In fact, in God's eyes, they could be considered far worse than the abrasive lady.*[9] To prejudge and cut someone off, as they have done, cannot be condoned. Such rejection is anathema to authentic discipleship. It is elitist, pure and simple.

I have this feeling that their rejection extends to far more than her "porcupine" personality. Essentially, they dislike her because they've concluded that she's basically inferior. Unworthy. A loser.

And that's a reflection on them. Dan Reeves had it right when he stated, "You can tell the character of a man by the way he treats those who can do nothing for him."

But here is the tragedy of the situation: This lady has no possible way of overcoming their adverse judgment. Even the most compassionate actions on her part can never reverse their opinion or earn their respect. In their book, she's doomed because of what they perceive her to be.

Under such conditions, I am not certain how many of us would have her kind of courage. Our predominant reactions would likely be: "What's the use?" "What do I have to gain?" "I might as well toss in the towel."

---

9. *Life Application Bible: New Testament,* lists these "wrongs" associated with showing favoritism:
   A. It is inconsistent with Christ's teachings.
   B. It results from evil thoughts.
   C. It belittles people made in God's image.
   D. It is a by-product of selfish motives.
   E. It goes against the biblical definition of love.
   F. It shows a lack of mercy to those less fortunate.
   G. It is hypocritical.
   H. It is sin.

3. Those who have continued to affirm this lady, like my wife, deserve credit. They have had to courageously overlook the elitists—who consider them "guilty by association."

My father used to say: Doing good, while receiving criticism from "good" people, is like "building the wagon and carrying the load at the same time."

It seems as if those people who refuse to extend arms of love would refrain from attacking those who do. Perhaps being personally uninvolved may predispose them to such negative attitudes. Maybe, in actuality, they are being consistently uncompassionate!

Nevertheless their actions are an increased burden on the shoulders of the compassionate—and a serious affront to our Saviour who embodies loving compassion.

Flipping Over the Coin

Granted, compassion is interwoven with Christian discipleship. Granted, compassion is not optional—it's a necessity. Granted, to claim to be "one of His," and to portray a lack of compassion, is serious business. Granted, compassion requires true courage.

Looking at the positive side of the coin, compassion gives luster and brilliance to our lives. It is the gateway to meaningful, significant living. Furthermore, it is but an outward overflow of Christ's Spirit that reigns within. For that reason it should come naturally when our lives are aligned with His will.

But don't get me wrong. The results of compassion are not always instantly apparent. Often there must be time for our "compassion seeds" to germinate. We must be patient, as we anticipate the harvest.

Also, compassion always has a high price. It never comes easily, nor should we approach it with a cavalier attitude. In his inimitable style, C.S. Lewis explains:

> Love anything, and your heart will certainly be wrung and possibly broken. If you want to [keep] it intact, you must give your heart to no one. . . . Wrap it carefully around with hobbies and little luxuries, avoid all entanglements;

lock it up safe in the casket . . . of your selfishness. But in that casket—safe, dark, motionless, airless—it will change. It will not be broken; it will become unbreakable, impenetrable, irredeemable. . . . The only place outside heaven where you can be perfectly safe from all the dangers . . . of love is hell.[10]

In spite of its risks, compassion is well worth the price. Recently, I read a story that reassured me of this fact. I hope that it will speak to you, as it did to me.

He Had to Reach Up to Touch Bottom

Jesus said, "I tell you the truth, whatever you [do] for the least of these brothers of mine, you [do] for me" (Matt. 25:40).

Ted Stallard undoubtedly qualifies as the one of "the least." Turned off by school. Very sloppy in appearance. Expressionless. Unattractive. Even his teacher, Miss Thompson, enjoyed bearing down her red pen—as she placed Xs beside his many wrong answers.

If only she had studied his records more carefully. They read:

1st grade: Ted shows promise with his work and attitude, but (has) poor home situation.
2nd grade: Ted could do better. Mother seriously ill. Receives little help from home.
3rd grade: Ted is good boy but too serious. He is a slow learner. His mother died this year.
4th grade: Ted is very slow, but well-behaved. His father shows no interest whatsoever.

Christmas arrived. The children piled elaborately wrapped gifts on their teacher's desk. Ted brought one too. It was wrapped in brown paper and held together with Scotch Tape.

Miss Thompson opened each gift, as the children crowded

---

10. Johnston, *Walls or Bridges,* p. 63.

around to watch. Out of Ted's package fell a gaudy rhinestone bracelet, with half of the stones missing, and a bottle of cheap perfume.

The children began to snicker. But she silenced them by splashing some of the perfume on her wrist, and letting them smell it. She put the bracelet on too.

At day's end, after the other children had left, Ted came by the teacher's desk and said, "Miss Thompson, you smell just like my mother. And the bracelet looks real pretty on you. I'm glad you like my presents." He left.

Miss Thompson got down on her knees and asked God to forgive her and to change her attitude.

The next day, the children were greeted by a reformed teacher—one committed to loving each of them. Especially the slow ones. Especially Ted.

Surprisingly—or maybe, not surprisingly, Ted began to show great improvement. He actually caught up with most of the students and even passed a few.

Graduation came and went. Miss Thompson heard nothing from Ted for a long time. Then, one day, she received this note:

Dear Miss Thompson:
I wanted you to be the first to know.
I will be graduating second in my class.
Love, Ted

Four years later, another note arrived:

Dear Miss Thompson:
They just told me I will be graduating first in my class. I wanted you to be first to know.
The university has not been easy, but I liked it.
Love, Ted.

And four years later:

Dear Miss Thompson:
As of today, I am Theodore Stallard, M.D. How about that? I wanted you to be the first to know.

I am getting married next month, the 27th to be exact. I want you to come and sit where my mother would sit if she were alive. You are the only family I have now; Dad died last year.

Miss Thompson attended that wedding, and sat where Ted's mother would have sat. The compassion she had shown that young man entitled her to that privilege.

Let's have some real courage, and start giving to "one of the least." He may become a Ted Stallard. Even if that doesn't happen, we will have been faithful to the One who has always treated us—as unworthy as we are—like *very special people.*[11]

---

11. Charles R. Swindoll, *The Quest for Character* (Portland, Ore.: Multnomah Press, 1987), pp. 178-181.

CHAPTER NINE

Relinquishing the Security Blanket:
Courage Is Risk

"Security is like the side of a swimming pool. We can use it to cling to or to push off from." (Terry Sullivan)

"Courage is grace under pressure." (Ernest Hemingway)

"Leave the irreparable past in His Hands, and step out into the irresistible future with Him." (Oswald Chambers)

A silver jet pierced the azure sky. Suddenly, it reached a large mass of dark, billowing storm clouds. The airplane was jolted from side to side. Drinks spilled. Babies started crying.

Let's pick up on an actual conversation between my author-friend, Tony Campolo, and the nun who trembled beside him.

Tony: Sister, can I say something to calm you?

Nun: (no response—continuing in a state of panic)

Tony: Sister, you should remember that Jesus said, "I am with you always."

Nun: Oh no He didn't! He said, "LO, I am with you always!"

Tony had to smile.

Have you ever been forced into a high-risk situation? I mean really high-risk—such as:

- being told that you must have a life-threatening operation;
- having to jump from one mountain cliff to another;
- needing to enter a building which has just received a bomb threat.

For most of us, risk-taking isn't our favorite pastime. It makes our hearts race. Our knuckles turn white. Our minds worry. Usually, we only take risks when we see no other alternative—when we're boxed into a corner.

Safety and security are a top priority. That's why we "buckle-up," run to the medicine cabinet when scratched, and make certain that our drinking water is pure.

And that's why we avoid tackling formidable enemies. We'd rather avoid or flee from bullies. As one person put it, it's better to be a live coward than a dead hero. Another echoed the same sentiment: Sissies live longer.[1]

But though our natural inclinations pull us in the direction of security, we know a life of hyper-caution is one of insignificance. Robert Louis Stevenson indicted the attitude of safety and prudence as "that dismal fungus."[2]

The truth is plain: More failure is the result of excess caution than of bold experimentation with new ideas. Without sufficient daring our lives will become failures.

Ask any salesperson. Whenever he or she ventures forth to push a product, there is plenty of risk involved. People are guaranteed to often say no. But to those who continue risking, the results are rewarding. One study on people in sales revealed that:

48 percent make only one call on the same person, then quit.
25 percent make two calls, then cease.
15 percent make three calls, then desist.
12 percent make four or more calls—but they earn 80 percent of all profit.[3]

Allow me to stop and make a qualification. I am not making an appeal for impulsive recklessness. Even for risk takers,

---

1. Another, more familiar, way of stating this principle: *He who fights and runs away lives to fight another day.*
2. "The Reaper," May 1961, p. 89. Quoted in J. Oswald Sanders, *Spiritual Leadership* (Chicago: Moody Press, 1967), p. 117.
3. These figures were quoted in a sermon. No source was supplied. It is also popular knowledge that the typical salesman hears forty noes to every one yes.

preventative measures and logical thinking are musts. It's just that once we're convinced that we should act, we must not be tentative.

As a child, I recall Davy Crockett advising, "Be sure you're right, then go ahead." He did. I should have followed that advice more than I have.

Realizing the good that can come to us through risk-taking, why do we remain tucked away in our nests of security?

The Spoilers

According to one author, many of us have attitudes that paralyze our thinking and lock us up in "Status Quo Penitentiary."

Here are the "mental locks" that keep us prisoners:

1. THE RIGHT ANSWER.
2. THAT'S NOT LOGICAL
3. FOLLOW THE RULES.
4. BE PRACTICAL.
5. AVOID AMBIGUITY.
6. TO ERR IS WRONG.
7. PLAY IS FRIVOLOUS.
8. THAT'S NOT MY AREA.
9. DON'T BE FOOLISH.
10. I'M NOT CREATIVE.[4]

The same author says that nothing less than a "whack on the side of the head" can dislodge these mind-sets.

I advise a "whack on the heart." It seems that little else can change entrenched attitudes. How does this "whack on the heart" happen? What kinds of perspectives must be cultivated? And what is the sequence of developing these perspectives?

To begin with, we must explore the *origins* of our mental inhibitors. By understanding their sources, we will discover clues which will help us disengage from these locked mind-sets. Essentially, they come from four sources, which can be

---

4. Roger von Oech, *A Whack on the Side of the Head* (New York: Warner Books, 1983), p. 9.

thought of as the "frowning prison guards" who guard our cells.

> *Source #1—Fear* (When we're scared to death, we have little appetite for chance-taking.)
> *Source #2—Perfectionism* (When it must always be done "correctly," we believe it's best to not risk failure.)
> *Source #3—Laziness* (When we lack energy, and slump back into atrophy, any "will to venture" dissipates.)
> *Source #4—Traditionalism* (To always "do it like our fathers did it" kills any risk taking.)[5]

When we buy into any of the above, we are consumed with a doubt that makes us unwilling to risk.

Nevertheless, we can encourage ourselves with hope. God can cause the doubt to disappear and replace it with a desire to venture forth.

These biblical heroes are cases in point. They triumphantly escaped their restricting doubts, and their *ventures* turned into victorious *adventures:*

Doubter	Doubtful moment	Reference
Abraham	When God told him he would be a father in old age	Genesis 17:17
Sarah	When she heard she would be a mother in old age	Genesis 18:12
Moses	When God told him to return to Egypt to lead the people	Exodus 3:10-15
Israelites	Whenever they faced difficulties in the wilderness	Exodus 16:1-3
Gideon	When told he would save Israel	Judges 6:14-23
Zechariah	When told he would be a father in old age	Luke 1:18
Thomas	When told Jesus had risen from the dead[6]	John 20:24-25

5. Charles R. Swindoll, *The Quest for Character* (Portland, Ore.: Multnomah Press, 1987), p. 200.
6. *Life Application Bible: New Testament,* Bruce Barton, ed. (Wheaton, Ill.: Tyndale House Publishers, Inc., and Youth For Christ/USA, 1987), p. 151.

These people of God, who became courageous venturers, started out as world-class doubters. But our Heavenly Father showed great patience with them. And His patience paid off.

Key point: Doubt is never a bad starting point, *if* we're not content to remain there.

Once we escape from the mental shackles and slip past these ever-watchful guards, we are free to begin dreaming.

Many of us get bogged down with nagging problems and responsibilities. As a result we remain mired in doubt. We neglect to dream.[7] And this is tragic. Why? Because little is ever accomplished that is not first envisioned. The writer of Proverbs puts it even more strongly: "Where there is no vision, the people perish" (Prov. 29:18, KJV).

Dreaming and vision, though commendable, are still not enough for those of us who follow the Man from Galilee. They weren't for Him. They're not for us.

You see, Jesus was much more than a visionary—He was a missionary! The difference lies in the nature of the dreaming.

Not Just Any Dream Will Do

Tyrants and unethical businessmen dream. So do murderers and thieves. I'm reminded of how the "Birdman of Alcatraz" was obsessed by his dream of escape. How Alexander the Great was consumed by his dream of conquest. How J. Paul Getty was driven by his desire to acquire wealth.

But we are different. Like Jesus, our aspirations must be tested by the litmus test of God's Word. Scripture accurately distinguishes between good and bad dreams.

And what is a good dream, according to the Bible? Allow me to paraphrase the words of Paul (Phil. 4:8): Whatever is *true,* whatever is *noble,* whatever is *right,* whatever is *pure,* whatever is *lovely,* whatever is *admirable*—we will *dream* on those things.

Elsewhere Paul declares, "Since, then, you have been raised with Christ, set your hearts on *things above . . .* not on earthly things" (Col. 3:1-2, italics added).

---

7. See Harold Ivan Smith, *No Fear of Trying: Turn Your "I've Always Wanted To" Wishes into Reality* (Nashville, Tenn.: Thomas Nelson Publishers), 1988.

The dreams of non-Christians stand in radical contrast to truth, rightness, purity, and the other spiritual qualities listed above. Instead, according to the apostle, they are likely to dream on things such as, "sexual immorality, impurity, lust, evil desires, and greed, which is idolatry" (vv. 5-6). Their focus is on pleasing themselves rather than God or others; "laying up treasures on earth" rather than in heaven; and climbing to the top of the "ladder"—even if it means pushing off others as they ascend.

Perhaps it's this perspective that keeps non-Christians from understanding what motivates Christians to risk for the right. To non-Christians, it seems incredibly foolish. They simply fail to see the value of the Christians' kind of dream.

Not long ago I heard a story that illustrates this incongruity more than any I've ever heard. Let me share it.

A Clash of Dreams

My friend, a minister in San Diego, recently took his son on a harbor cruise to celebrate the boy's twenty-first birthday. The ship was named "The Invader." It was custom-made in Quincy, Massachusetts, in 1905, for William Borden—founder of the milk company by that name.

The ship's captain explained that there were no heirs to assume ownership of the boat, thus, it was sold at public auction. That's how it ended up in San Diego.

In the week following his visit, Pastor Paul heard "the rest of the story." And he just had to share it with his congregation the next Sunday morning. I visited his service that day and shall never forget the story's impact on my own life.

The Bordens had a son who was given every advantage imaginable throughout his youth. Frequently, they reminded him that he was the person chosen to inherit the company. And that he should begin "grooming" himself for the awesome responsibility.

Then one day, it was off to college he went.

While there, some friends introduced him to Jesus Christ. That's when *everything* changed, especially his dreams!

He announced to his father that he would be relinquishing

his future in the company and becoming a missionary to the Orient.

The parents' shock was almost too much to bear. *What? Give up what most Americans dream about? Power. Status. Wealth. Possessions, including the luxurious family yacht. How ungrateful! How tragic! How incomprehensible!*

Mr. Borden scrambled to do all within his power to talk his son out of his "foolish" decision. He offered further enticements. He attempted to induce guilt. He even tried scare tactics, warning his son of a plague that was spreading through the Orient. But to no avail. The boy's mind was made up. He would follow *God's dream* for his life.

And so he departed.

After a few months, William Sr. received a letter from the missionary board. As he opened it, he thought to himself, *Has my son been honored in a special way? Better yet, are they informing me that he is coming home for good?*

Then, as he began reading, tears welled up in his eyes. His son had died. He had contracted the fatal disease.

Mr. Borden's intense sorrow soon turned to anger as he thought about "what might have been." If only.... If only....

The funeral came and went, but the sorrow remained. In fact, it intensified.

Then, some months later, a small package arrived in the mail. It was from another missionary who had been the son's close friend.

The letter inside spoke of their friendship, and the son's tremendous ministry. The letter concluded with this postscript: "Mr. Borden, you will find your son's Bible enclosed. It meant so much to him, and I know it will to you."

The milk magnate began to thumb through the Book he knew very little about. Then, just as he was about to close it, he noticed some words scratched on the back flyleaf. The date beside corresponded to the week before his son's death.

Upon closer inspection, he discovered that this was his son's own handwriting. His heart was overwhelmed, as he slowly and softly read to himself:

NO RESERVE
NO RETREAT
NO REGRET

The words were like sharp knives that punctured his cal-loused heart. Yet those words caused Mr. Borden to begin rethinking his priorities.

His son had a dream—a dream with eternal significance. In following that dream, the young man risked everything. But, in so doing, what he gained was immeasurable!

William Borden realized this now. Sure, he still grieved, yet he no longer grieved with resentment. Rather, his grief was tinged with deep respect.

An inspiring story, indeed. But many of us no doubt see William Borden, Jr.'s dream as beyond our comprehension. We assume that this guy was some sort of a saint. One-in-a-million. Very much unlike the rest of us. We aren't Borden heirs by a long shot. We're doing well just to keep milk on our tables!

Is there a way we can bring this business of "risk" down to where we live? I believe there is.

Our Nine-to-Five World

We must realize that "risking for Jesus" is a biblical assignment for all believers—whether we live in a mansion or a shanty. Whether we eat lobster three times a week or dine with the same frequency on beans and corn bread.

If we're truly Christians, we will risk. The Lord is counting on us. And the advancement of His kingdom on earth is at stake. It was H.W.K. Moule who rightly said, "The frontiers of the Kingdom of God were never advanced by men and women of caution."

Furthermore, our abandonment of security will be reward-ed. Jesus said so: "And everyone who has left houses or brothers or sisters or fathers or mothers or children or fields for my sake will receive a hundred times as much and will inherit eternal life" (Matt. 19:29).

We must begin to courageously risk *where* we are, *as* we

are, *whenever* we can. Or, as someone has aptly advised: We must immediately begin "blooming right where we're planted."

In what ways can we begin to risk? Here are a few suggestions:

- Dare to invite another to accept Jesus as his or her Saviour; Proverbs 11:30 declares "he who wins souls is wise."

- Put ourselves in environments where we're likely to be ridiculed for our faith (e.g., choosing to be a teetotaler at cocktail parties).

- Get to know someone whom others consider a real "turnoff" or "loser" (e.g., befriend someone who's trying to quit drugs).

- Lovingly confront someone who is unintentionally hurting another.

- Take on a high-risk project that is guaranteed to yield little public acclaim, and take its toll on your patience—something others feel is too far beneath them to undertake.

No doubt, all of us have other suggestions tailored to our own situations.

We know when we're playing it safe and opting for our own security and comfort. And, deep down, we know when and how we should stand up and be counted. I have to believe that because of a recent incident in my own life. Allow me to share it with you.

God's Office of Career Placement

Those of you who know me pretty well may have heard someone say, "Boy, Jon, you're pretty safe. You teach at that big, fancy university out west—and you're not encumbered by any denominational supervision or restriction."

Or maybe you've heard someone pipe up with, "Jon, you'll certainly never have to worry about your career. You can say or do anything you want."

To be honest, a part of me believed this. Until a year ago. That's when it was pointed out to me, by leaders in my denomination, that my career was in jeopardy—unless I shut up fast.

You see, there was this little problem with the leadership in my local church.

People are still telling me that I kept my "head in the sand" too long, because I didn't speak out sooner. I just didn't want to believe what was happening.

Was I ever naive!

Well, the Lord cleared it really fast in my mind—with some rather shocking evidence. And He told me that I would have to join in with those who were taking a stand.

I never questioned His voice, but like David of old, I seriously wondered if He had asked the right person.

I said, "Lord, this is a tough assignment. Can't You just take care of it Yourself?"

He said to me, "I'm counting on you, and I will be with you each step of the way."

So, I decided to contact the first denominational leader. After I explained the situation, he responded, "That's all well and good. We do need to do what's right. But, Jon, it seems like you're up on the ladder. You have earned a measure of respect in our denomination."

I looked shocked and replied, "I hadn't really given that much thought."

He replied, "Let me put it to you straight. If you stand up on this issue, I fear for your career."

We parted. And I passed off what he had said.

I had no option but to go all the way to the top—which meant flying out to talk with someone "higher up." When I finished my presentation, this man looked me straight in the eyes—in front of another board member—and said, "Jon, you know you're pretty much up there on the ladder."

"What exactly do you mean?" I asked.

He replied, "I mean that you could seriously harm your career."

I could take no more, and said, "If you've read my books, you know that my career is far less important to me than doing what the Lord asks me to do." He nodded.

Well, you probably are wondering what finally happened. To abbreviate this story, let me tell you that the whole situation was resolved. Our church was freed from the shadow of suspicion, deception, and intimidation. And with new leadership, after just one year, we have registered a thirty-three percent growth in every area.

Still, I'm quite sure that in the minds of some, my "respect, power, and recognition" have been damaged. But is that what really matters? Who cares about my career? Besides, after I said yes to Christ's assignment, it wasn't *my* career any longer.

Paraphrasing Mother Teresa, Senator Mark Hatfield recently said to our faculty, "It's not how *successful* we are, in the world or in the church's eye, but how *faithful* we are to the principles we know to be right."

CHAPTER TEN

In the Same Building, But on Another Floor: Courage Is Solitude

---

"Many of us, resolving to be courageous, resemble the mosquito that found himself in a nudist colony. He knew what to do; he just couldn't decide where to start!"

"Courage is almost a contradiction in terms. It means a strong desire to live taking the form of a readiness to die." (G.K. Chesterton)

"People whose character is being developed, stretched and deepened aren't hesitant to say 'Go' even though the majority say 'No.'" (Charles Swindoll)

Mrs. Carlo Ponti, does the name ring a bell? You may know her better as Sophia Loren—world-renowned star of over one hundred films.

I had heard about her moving to Southern California, and her son, Carlo Ponti, Jr. enrolling in our university.

One day the boy dropped by my office to sign up for our China trip. His father, famous producer of such films as *Doctor Zhivago*, accompanied him. They were very cordial and easy to talk with.

Before leaving my office, they asked if my wife and I might possibly agree to come to their house for dinner. Sophia wanted to meet the people who would be taking her son halfway around the world.

Excited about the prospect, but trying to look composed, I

assured them that we could probably manage to work it into our schedule.

The next week I was doing some work at my office when the phone rang. It was Sophia herself calling to confirm a time. Her voice was warm as she furnished the directions.

On the appointed evening we drove to the Ponti estate. We were welcomed at the front door by the maid who invited us to be seated in the living room. We were impressed by the simple elegance of the decor.

Carlo Ponti and his son came in. They were both friendly, and we laughed at stories about their dog, snacked on hors d'oeuvres, and discussed our plans for the upcoming trip.

Then Sophia entered. As beautiful as you might imagine, we instantly found her personality to be equally as attractive. She was an excellent conversationalist, passing off any references to her many successes and expressing an interest in our lives.

Before long, we were eating dinner at a marble table that overlooked a beautiful garden. The dinner lasted three hours, though it seemed like only ten minutes or so. Carlo and Sophia teased each other. They asked questions about our university, the state of affairs in China, and a host of other things—such as the feasability of using tapes to improve self-confidence while asleep. Concerning the latter, I recall suggesting the reading of Scripture instead.

Sophia told about her mother in Italy, whom she telephones every day. Then she described her other son, who attends school in Switzerland.

There was no name-dropping. No put-downs. No "show biz" talk. No bragging about achievements or awards. Just good old-fashioned conversation about things we're all interested in: family, values, humorous moments of embarrassment, etc.

Through it all, Sophia Loren was the perfect hostess—constantly making sure that we were enjoying our food.

The time came to depart. Sophia walked with us to the front room, where she autographed two or three of her books. She quietly handed them to my wife Cherry.

We said our good-byes, and went out the front door. Our

gracious hostess stood and watched us as we descended the steps to our car. When we looked back, she waved.

The trip to China went very well. And I wasn't surprised to observe that Carlo, Jr. was a perfect gentleman throughout. It was very evident that his caring parents had instilled worthwhile principles in his life.

Of course, after our close contact, I was very interested to read Mrs. Ponti's autobiography—a story of challenge and courage in difficult circumstances.

More than Meets the Eye

Sophia was born in Pozzuoli, Italy. Her father abandoned the family and she grew up an illegitimate, impoverished slum urchin. At school, she was mercilessly teased about her illegitimacy.

Then, Nazi soldiers invaded her town. They stole from the people and drew attacks from Allied troops. In one bombing raid, Sophia was hit by shrapnel. When the war started going badly for Germany, she witnessed the Nazi soldiers killing her neighbors.

After the war, Sophia's personal "war" continued. She tried learning to play the piano, but quit because her mother banged her over the head when she made mistakes. Overcoming all the obstacles, she managed to break into films.

She met, and lived with, Carlo—who was older than she— and whom she considered security-giver, father-image, and lover. The Vatican denounced her as a "public sinner," because Ponti was married at the time.

Finally, after his divorce, they were married. Trials continued—including a series of miscarriages, a robbery, and finally, a mix-up in taxes which led to the Italian government issuing a warrant for Sophia's arrest.

In spite of her difficulties, Sophia continued to make films, and to impress the world with her beauty and talent. In time, she and Carlo had two healthy sons and moved to America.

At this point in the book, I surmised that all the bad times were behind her. Sophia could now take a well-deserved deep breath and truly enjoy life.

Well, life isn't like that for the famous. They never escape the penetrating public eye. Or disregard the possibility of some deranged killer stalking their path.[1] In short, they must isolate themselves. The result: loneliness.

Toward the end of the book, Carlo Ponti, Sr. describes his wife as "antisocial." There could be no spur-of-the-moment dinners in a nearby restaurant, or a night on the town. Why? "The moment we put our feet out of the [house], we are molested by the public. . . . When we go out, we are curiosities. The press assaults us, and outrageously distorts what they write about us."

He goes on, "We mostly avoid parties because if we go to one person's house, then others are miffed if we don't go to theirs."

He concludes, "Some feel that Sophia does not have fun, is not enjoying her life, because she stays home so much. But they don't realize what an ordeal it is when she does go out."

Then, these telling words: *"She is a prisoner when she goes out, and free to be herself only when she's behind her own four walls."*[2]

The Flip Side of Fame

What is true about Sophia Loren is true for all who distinguish themselves from the masses. They simply stand out. They are visible.

We see this especially in the lives of our U.S. Presidents. As one writer declared, "Loneliness stalks where the buck stops."

---

1. "John Lennon turned toward the voice in the dark; actress Rebecca Schaeffer responded to a knock on her door. Both were gunned down on their own doorsteps by obsessed, disturbed fans." Lennon's killer is described as a "suicidal loner who drew inspiration from *The Catcher in the Rye*, J.D. Salinger's novel of adolescent angst." Schaeffer's killer allegedly hired a private detective agency to track down the actress. When celebrities are murdered, Hollywood draws the curtains and pays thousands for beefed-up protection. Lennon's murder in 1980 frightened former Beatles drummer, Ringo Starr, into hiring five security guards.
Bob Groves, *Los Angeles Examiner*, August 3, 1989, pp. B1, 4.
2. A.E. Hotchner, *Sophia Living and Loving: Her Own Story* (New York: William Morrow and Company, Inc., 1979), p. 224.

Consider Abraham Lincoln. Today we're convinced of his greatness, but on the day he died Lincoln's critics were numerous and fierce. He endured a lonely agony that reflected our country's turmoil—just after being ripped to shreds by a cruel and costly Civil War.

On the night he was assassinated, at Ford Theatre, these items were removed from Lincoln's pockets:

- handkerchief, embroidered "A. Lincoln";
- farm boy's pocketknife;
- purse, containing $5 *Confederate* bill;
- spectacles case, held together by a string;
- and some old, worn newspaper clippings.

The clippings told of his great deeds. One reported a speech by John Bright, which said Lincoln is "one of the greatest men of all times." It seems touchingly pathetic that this "man for the ages" had to seek self-assurance from a few old newspaper clippings. See him as he reads them under the candle's flickering flame—all alone—in the Oval Office.[3] He's the picture of loneliness.

This type of loneliness is also true of sports personalities. When they perform well, they are considered heroes. But when they are in a slump, the "boo birds" come out. Suddenly, those who received cheers only a few days before, experience the intense loneliness that accompanies rejection.

In addition to loneliness are the threats. When former Los Angeles Dodger pitcher, Joe Moeller, spoke to my Community Organization class, he said players constantly receive threatening phone calls and death threats from "sickies." Menacing voices say things like: "Don't plan on playing another game after tonight. There will be a gun pointed at your temple in the third inning."

The point is clear: To become *visible* in the public eye is to become *vulnerable*. You become vulnerable to abuse. Vulnerable to attack. Vulnerable to invasion of privacy. And as a result, vulnerable to the pangs of loneliness.

---

3. Charles R. Swindoll, *The Quest for Character* (Portland, Ore.: Multnomah Press, 1987), p. 62.

Facing the world, with that extreme kind of vulnerability, requires great courage.

A Timeless Principle

This reality is not confined to today. It has existed since mankind began singling out individuals for special attention.

One sociologist refers to such individuals as "marginal." They seem to be, at best, bigger-than-life, and at worst, they appear abnormal. Somehow, they avoid categories.[4]

When these people become famous we term them "celebrities." When they are perceived as infamous we call them "deviants."[5] In either case, they simply don't fit in with others. Like brown shoes with a black tuxedo. As a result, they are treated differently. So differently that they often feel compelled to retreat into the safety and serenity of their own solitude.

When persons become visible, or "poke their heads above the crowd," they are singled out for special attention. So much so that they are forced to *isolate* or *insulate* themselves.[6] When that occurs, intense loneliness is the result.

What does this have to do with courage? Simply this: Many around us hesitate to take courageous stands. They take the way of least resistance. If they do take a stand, their courage relates to an area of little consequence—a "tempest in a teapot" (e.g., arguing politics). Or they stand firm in an area that concerns self-gratification (e.g., crowding in line).

---

4. See Everett V. Stonequist, *The Marginal Man* (New York: C. Scribner's Sons, 1937).
5. In one social psychological experiment, the effects of even minor deviation are demonstrated. Ten groups were formed to solve various issues. All members were paid. In each group, a confederate (i.e., person assigned to do or say something in order to make this an experiment) was appointed. He was asked to subtly disagree with the group consensus. The second time around, researchers told participants that they were running short of funds and must eliminate one member per group. Wishing to be democratic, group members would vote on the person that should be eliminated. In all ten groups, the wave-making confederate was eliminated!
6. Isolation refers to removing oneself spatially. Putting distance between oneself and others. Insulation means remaining close, but shutting off oneself from others—by becoming truly different or distinct (in the manner of dress, speech pattern, religious rituals, etc.).

When we, as followers of Jesus, are courageous on issues that really count, we set ourselves apart like speckled birds in a single-color flock. We are perceived as nonconformists. People notice that we're not marching in lockstep to this world's drummer and often it bugs them.

Try not swearing around those who do. Or refusing an alcoholic beverage when others are imbibing. Or not laughing at a smutty story—or ethnic joke.

In a more positive way, visibly interact with people that others consider to be "pure trash" or "hopeless." Express the need for compassion for those who are afflicted with AIDS. Bow your head to say grace before a meal.

All of these actions prompt others to think of us as special, different, or just plain weird. We will stand out in their minds and be plopped into a category they title "other." Once categorized in this manner, we can be sure of being treated differently. Perhaps some people will show greater respect. But most, because of guilt, fear, or pure discomfort, will dispense varying degrees of ostracism. This will show itself through silence, stares, snide comments, and the like.

How are we likely to feel? Pretty lonely. We'll feel cutoff—like we're traveling our own road. We won't be sure of being understood—even by other Christians or our families. We won't know if we are truly *liked* or if we are merely being *tolerated.*

Are there instances of courageous Christian personalities who were subject to these sentiments? Let's consider a few. Perhaps, they'll help us to be better able to cope with our loneliness.

They Carried the Torch—Lighted
Courageous biblical leaders remained faithful throughout their solitude.

Moses was alone on the mount and alone in the plain. He experienced the crushing loneliness of misunderstanding, unfair criticism, and questioning of motive. He had no close chums—no real confidants.

The *prophets* were the loneliest of men. Enoch walked alone in a decadent society, as he proclaimed impending judgment. So did Elijah, Isaiah, Amos, and Hosea.

Hear *Jeremiah* as he says, "Alas, my mother, that you gave me birth, a man with whom the whole land strives and contends! I have neither lent nor borrowed, yet everyone curses me" (Jer. 15:10).

Who could have experienced pangs of loneliness more than *Jonah?* He courageously proclaimed the message of imminent judgment to a heathen city of a million persons. But prior to this, it wasn't exactly "party time" in the stomach of that big fish!

Daniel stood tall. After being threatened with death for worshiping God, he intentionally prayed aloud through an open window. His enemies heard, tattled, and rejoiced as he was taken to the lions' den.

Feel marginal? No loneliness we experience today could compare with what he must have felt as he stared at the bicuspids of those beasts.

Sure, *David* had a remarkable friendship with Jonathan—but only in his early years. When he became Israel's king, his greatest battles, deepest prayers, and hardest decisions had to be made in solitude.

Then there is the gregarious *Paul* who experienced the bitterness of being misunderstood by contemporaries, misrepresented by his enemies, and deserted by his converts and friends.

Catch the pathos of his voice as he declares to Timothy, "This thou knowest, that all they which are in Asia be turned away from me" (2 Tim. 1:15, KJV).[7]

Moving to more contemporary times, let's eavesdrop on retiring missionary, Hudson Taylor, as he explains the China Inland Mission assignment to his successor, *Dixon Hoste.*

We see Dixon's somber countenance, as the weight of responsibility is unloaded onto his shoulders. He thinks to himself: "Can one man be courageous enough to carry this load?"

---

7. J. Oswald Sanders, *Spiritual Leadership: A Timely and Practical Guide to Working Effectively with People* (Chicago: Moody Press, 1967), pp. 107-108.

The important meeting draws to a close. Those standing nearby hear missionary Hoste's final words, as he leaves Taylor's presence, "And now I have no one, no one but God!"

A.W. Tozer puts it straight: "Most of the world's great souls have been lonely. Loneliness seems to be the price a saint must pay for his saintliness."[8]

The bottom line is this: Today's courageous Christian must be someone who, while welcoming friendship and support of all who offer, has sufficient inner resources to stand alone—even to face fierce opposition—in obeying the Lord.

F.W.H. Meyers puts these sentiments in verse:

On without cheer of sister or of daughter,
Yes, without stay of father or of son,
Lone on the land, and homeless on the water,
Pass I in patience till my work be done.[9]

If loneliness is inevitable for those of us who choose to be courageous, we must have certain attitudes to help us cope. Let's examine some of these.

S.O.S. Kit for Lonely Stalwarts

Attitudes, defined by sociologists as our "learned inclinations to respond," can be powerful.

Situations that are perceived as negative and even hopeless by most, can be perceived as springboards to opportunity. It's the old "let's turn our lemons into lemonade" idea—and it works. Especially, as applied to that kind of loneliness that results from taking courageous stands.

What attitudes should be tucked away in our survival kit? Let's look at these, master them, and draw from them often.

1. Always remember that ours is a "chosen" loneliness.

Many are lonely simply because they allow themselves to be "processed" by our impersonal, automated society. Switchboards, traffic jams, mass media, computers, junk mail, and a

---

8. Ibid., p. 108.
9. Ibid.

host of other things that are encountered daily, can take their toll. People begin to feel overpowered. Like a "cog" in society's wheel.

But our loneliness is because we have chosen to take courageous stands. Thus, we willfully say yes to the lonely pathway. Not because we are victimized, but rather, because we wish to be victors!

That thought should help us to stand taller and feel better.

2. We must accept our loneliness without "excess baggage."

Once we gain ascendency over being depressed about our loneliness, there is the ever-present temptation to allow it to collect additional attitudinal weight. Let me explain.

We can accept our loneliness, but permit it to make us increasingly bitter or resentful. It becomes a "badge" to remind ourselves how bad we have it. And we have frequent "black-tie pity parties."

Also, our solitude can be attached to an attitude of self-righteousness. We can feel that our "cross" qualifies us for heavenly (and even earthly) VIP status.

These attitudes must be soundly rejected. Instead, we must bear our loneliness with quiet dignity—just as our Saviour did when He stood accused before Pilate.

3. As our courage is God's gift, so our loneliness is borne by His grace.

We must remember that, though we may be lonely, we are never really alone. He is always with us.

Separated from the clamoring voices of others, we are better able to hear His voice. Without needing to conform to the demands of others, we are better able to follow His will. Our intimacy with Him can be accentuated because, in reality, it's just us and our Maker.

Charles Swindoll employs just the right words: "It is in lonely solitude that God delivers His best thoughts."[10]

Undeniably, our human nature craves company. It is only natural to want to share with others. To be in solitude is discomforting, especially for the Christian. But our loneliness

---

10. Swindoll, op. cit., p. 63.

need not hamstring us. With the attitudes above, we will emerge victorious. And what appears to others to be an impediment can actually become a source of strength.

Just as the ground that lies fallow enriches itself for the next planting, so our solitude can be a period of spiritual nourishment—readying us for a future challenge.

Again, it comes down to the battery of attitudes we choose to embrace. Unfortunately, some have selected negative attitudes and have succumbed. Though tragic, their stories can teach us important lessons.

The Dark Clouds Gathered

Few stories have made me sadder than that of Bob Pierce, founder of World Vision International. Most of us know this organization to be, perhaps, the largest Christian relief effort to Third World countries. Much of the World Vision success is due to Bob's wise leadership.

At the time of its inception, there were no other programs of its kind. Skeptics, inside and outside the church, doubted its value. And they let Bob Pierce know of their misgivings.

But Bob was a special person. His courage was unbelievable. He was a man of prayer, faith, and action. Once he was convinced that World Vision was God's will, there was no stopping him.

Many closed doors had to be pushed open. Money-raising was resented by some church leaders—viewed as "taking money from the church." Efforts to improve the quality of life (by digging wells or planting crops) were seen as unworthy. Some felt that Christians should only be preaching to these people.

Bob felt the impact of the criticism and questions, but he just kept marching forward. And it was a very lonely march.

In a radio interview, his daughter stated that he became "married to his job." He was gone weeks, and even months, at a time. As a result, he became a "stranger" in his own home.

Then one of Bob's children committed suicide. And his wife reached her limit of the pressures in the marriage. She and Bob were separated.

It became evident that Bob Pierce was steadily sinking under the stress in his life and work. He even had a violent disagreement with his own board and resigned. (I warned you that this story was very sad.)

What a sorrowful picture. Here's the man who had courageously launched a great Christian organization. He had won hundreds, perhaps thousands, of souls to the Lord. Even the leaders of Third World countries respected him. Yet now we visualize him as an extremely lonely man—at a time in his life when he should have been inundated with friends and intimately involved with family.

It is not for us to know or judge the causes of Bob's difficulties. Yes, he achieved many accomplishments for God's kingdom, but somewhere along the line, this great leader lost his perspective.

Courage? He had an inordinate quantity, and he pushed back many of Satan's frontiers. But unlike Moses and David, when the inevitable loneliness came to him, he was unable to cope. He walled himself in, developed unhealthy attitudes, saw his "empire" collapse, and his family fragment.

Bob Pierce did gain a measure of serenity before his death. In fact, there was a brief family reunion at the hospital in Switzerland. It is also evident that the work he started continues in grand fashion.

Thus, his was not a wasted life—just one that was extremely lonely. And somehow he was unable to effectively cope within the confines of that solitude.

May we learn from his mistakes and accept our loneliness with patience and even thanksgiving.

Like Noah of old, let's courageously continue "building the boat," even though we're doing it ourselves. And even though others don't seem to understand.

CHAPTER ELEVEN

Going to the Mat:
Courage Is Commitment

"No problem facing our nation is so awesome, so complicated or so fraught with danger that the average citizen can't run away from it." (Charlie Brown, Peanuts comic strip)

"Whatever you can do, or dream you can, begin it. Boldness has genius, power and magic in it." (Goethe)

"If the trumpet does not sound a clear call, who will get ready for battle?" (1 Cor. 14:8)

I recently heard a tongue-in-cheek speech to graduating seniors, which highlighted the contrast between "cushy" college life and the harsh world of employment. It was entitled "Ten Reasons *Not* to Get a Job." Some of those reasons mentioned were:

- Your social life will be in shambles, because you'll need to get to bed at a decent hour.
- A job will prevent you from getting up late, watching favorite daytime soaps, and taking those long afternoon naps.
- Aware of your earning potential, your parents will charge you rent to live in "your room," and your alumni association and church will expect generous offerings.
- Unlike college, you'll have no excused absences, "free" days to go to the beach, or permission to sleep through sessions.

- Worst of all, if you get a job, most likely, *you'll have to go to work.*[1]

Working at a job requires commitment—as does getting married, joining the armed services, buying a hamster, keeping up an automobile, and (let me add) pursuing a college career.

Commitment is closely intertwined with courage. Commitment implies courage to take on a challenge, or having the courage to plow through obstacles along the way. Commitment includes courage to back off, when time and experience prove such commitments to have been unwise.

The dictionary defines commitment as "pledging oneself" to "a thing, idea or person."[2] I like Lewis Smedes' definition better: "learning to live the love we promise."[3]

Commitment carries with it the idea of giving time, energy, and other resources in a total, hands-down manner. Mere *involvement*, by contrast, is less intense and sacrificial. As someone aptly put it: "A chicken was *involved* in my breakfast. She laid the egg. But a pig was truly *committed*. He furnished the bacon."

What are the results of being really committed? Let's begin by spotlighting the secular world.

The Gateway to Significance

A study was recently completed on corporate managers. In it they were asked if they voiced positions that 1. focused on the good of the company, rather than personal benefit and 2. jeopardized their own careers.

Emerging from this study were the four leader-types which are found in all organizations.

---

1. Presented by Nancy Magnussun-Fagan at a breakfast to graduating seniors. Taken from the article, entitled "Ten Reasons Not to Get a Job" from the *Harvard Lampoon Big Book of College Life.*
2. *The Random House Dictionary,* Jess Stein, ed., "Commitment" (New York: Ballantine Books, 1980), p. 184.
3. Lewis B. Smedes, *Caring and Commitment: Learning to Live the Love We Promise* (San Franciso, Calif.: Harper and Row, Publishers, 1988).

Type #1—courageous. These people expressed ideas to help the company improve, in spite of personal risk or opposition.

Type #2—confronting. These people spoke up, but only because of a personal vendetta against the company.

Type #3—calloused. These people didn't know, or care, whether they could do anything for the company; they felt helpless and hopeless, so they kept quiet.

Type #4—conforming. These people also remained quiet, but only because they loathed confrontation and loved approval.[4]

The researchers discovered that the courageous managers accomplished the most, reported the highest job satisfaction, and eventually were commended by superiors. Their commitment had certainly improved the quality of their lives.

Commitment always pays off. Why? Because it causes us to initiate, rather than to passively await our fate. Commitment "jump starts" our lives!

W.H. Murray put it so well:

... Until one is committed there is hesitancy, the chance to draw back, always ineffectiveness. Concerning all acts of initiative (and creation), there is one elementary truth, the ignorance of which kills countless ideas and splendid plans: that *the moment one definitely commits oneself, then providence moves too.*

"All sorts of things occur to help one that would never otherwise have occurred. A whole stream of events issues from the decision, raising in one's favor all manner of unforeseen incidents and meetings and material assistance, which no man would have dreamt would have come his way.[5]

---

4. "When Corporate Courage Counts: During Hard Times, Business Is in Special Need of Lionhearted Management," by Harvey A. Hornstein, *Psychology Today,* September 1986, pp. 56, 58-60.

5. This quote, by W.H. Murray, is from an uncirculated sheet of paper that the author found. No source was indicated.

This is illustrated in a story shared by radio commentator, Earl Nightengale. A psychiatrist interviewed a number of skilled mountain climbers, just prior to their attempts to climb Mount Everest, asking each, "Will you get to the top?"

The psychiatrist received a variety of responses: "We'll have to wait and see." "I'm going to give it my best shot." "I just hope I'm lucky."

But one man of slight build had a totally different answer. He softly but emphatically responded, *"Yes, I will."*

Not surprisingly, he was the first to make it to the peak. "Yes, I will"—three of the most potent words in our language. Words of commitment. Words that make possibilities realities. And these are words usually spoken through the lips of truly courageous persons.

But for Christians, the commitments we make are much more praiseworthy than the kinds made by businessmen and mountain climbers. Our focus rises far above monetary profit and personal achievement. Furthermore, our commitment requires much greater courage.

Primarily, we commit ourselves to a *Person,* to *people,* and to crucial *principles.* Let's closely examine each area.

Commitment to Him, Our Highest Purpose

As previously mentioned, commitment to Jesus means taking on His identity. (See Galatians 2:20.) Ironically, after doing so, we become our true selves—with self-concepts that are *healthy* as well as *holy.*

I'll be a little more specific. There is, what Augustine has termed, a "God-shaped void" in all of us. This empty space can only be filled by Christ's presence.

Francis A. Schaeffer explains it this way:

It is impossible even to begin living the Christian life, or to know anything of true spirituality, before one is a Christian, and the only way to become a Christian is neither by trying . . . nor by hoping, but rather by *accepting Christ as Savior.* No matter how complicated, educated, or sophisticated we may be, or how simple we may

140

be, we must all come the same way. . . . This is true for all men, everywhere, through all space and all time. There are no exceptions. Jesus said a totally exclusive word: "No man cometh unto the Father but by Me" (John 14:6).[6]

Be assured, Jesus Christ will never impose His will on ours. He quietly stands at the door of our hearts and knocks. (See Revelation 3:20.) It's up to us to open and ask Him to enter. The door latch is on the inside!

We "open the door" to Jesus by acknowledging our sin (Romans 3:23), as well as its damaging effects (Romans 6:23). Then, we must ask our Saviour to remove that sin from our lives. We do that by confessing it to Him (1 John 1:9), in the act of repentance.[7]

Then, believing that His sacrifice on the Cross makes it possible for our sins to be removed (John 3:16; Romans 10:9-10), we must also believe that He has completed the work in our own lives. In short, we must reach up in faith—and claim His promises as our own.

The writer of Hebrews nails down the final step of faith in these emphatic words: "Anyone who comes to Him must believe that He exists and that He rewards those who earnestly seek Him" (Heb. 11:6).

In short, our commitment to Jesus must be the no-holds-barred kind. Total. Complete.

The result of this kind of commitment is that each one can become a new person. Paul declares, "Therefore, if anyone is in Christ, he is a *new* creation; the old has gone, the *new* has come" (2 Cor. 5:17, italics added).

We are wise, indeed, if we dedicate a lifetime to closely

---

6. This clipping, entitled "True Spirituality," had no source indicated.
7. There are two Greek verbs used for "repent" in the New Testament. Both pertain to sin. The first, *metamelomai,* connotes regret, remorse or sorrow for past wrong (see Matt. 21:29; 2 Cor. 7:10). The second, *metanoeo,* implies a change of mind or purpose—a change that is always for the better. A turning from sin, and a turning to God. In short, an about-face! (W.E. Vine, *An Expository Dictionary of New Testament Words* (Old Tappan, N.J.: Fleming H. Revell Company, 1966), pp. 279-280.

scrutinizing this One who gives us our new lease on life. Let's pause a moment to gaze at a few snapshots from His earthly scrapbook. See Him as He:

- stills the raging storm—demonstrating His awesome power;
- bids children come and sit on His lap—disclosing His protection of the weak and powerless;
- remains silent before Pilate—showing His reaction to attack;
- prays in the Garden of Gethsemane—revealing His total obedience to God.

After seeing these, many of us are tempted to say to ourselves: *We can never hope to be all that Jesus was. He fulfilled 60 Old Testament prophecies. He was the very Son of God, who was present at the time of man's creation.*

Napoleon spoke the truth when he concluded: "I know men. And Jesus was more than a man."

But, as perfect as He was, our Lord is still within our reach—or should I say *we* are in *His* reach. Though we can never *be* Christ, we can *do* things that He did, such as feeding the hungry, comforting the bereaved, confronting the powerful, or teaching God's Word in simple words.

Furthermore, once we commit our hearts to Him, we will sense a surge of strength within. As Paul put it: We will be "strengthened with all power according to His glorious might so that you may have great endurance and patience" (Col. 1:11).

For these reasons, Jesus is first and foremost the genesis of our commitment. It all begins with Him, but it certainly doesn't end there. After fully committing ourselves to Him, we'll find that other important commitments come spontaneously.

Let's look at two types of commitment that God highly values.

Commitment to People, Our Special Mission
Mother Teresa has stated that today our worst disease isn't leprosy or tuberculosis. In her words:

The greatest evil is the lack of love and charity, the terrible indifference toward one's neighbor who lives at the roadside assaulted by exploitation, corruption, poverty and disease.[8]

All of us, even Christians, are prone to get sucked up in the speed, technology, and craziness of the age—at the expense of revealing such love. Virginia Brasier puts it this way:

Time of the Mad Atom
This is the age
Of the half-read page.
And the quick hash
And the mad dash.
The bright night
With the nerves tight.
The plane hop
With the brief stop.
The lamp tan
In a short span.
The Big Shot
In a good spot.
And the brain strain
And the heart pain.
And the cat naps
Till the spring snaps—
And the fun's done![9]

(Reprinted from *The Saturday Evening Post,* © 1949, The Curtis Publishing Co.)

But even those of us who make time for commitments to persons often fail. And, as Lewis Smedes says, it's often for the same reasons.

We commit too quickly. We commit before we (or the other person) are mature. We commit with unrealistic expectations. We commit while "drunk" on romantic love. We commit with a

---

8. Ted W. Engstrom, *The Fine Art of Friendship* (Nashville, Tenn.: Thomas Nelson Publishers, 1985), p. 68.
9. From *Saturday Evening Post,* May 28, 1949, p. 72. Seen in Engstrom, op. cit., p. 73.

wretched self-image. We commit without knowing how to effectively communicate.[10]

Perhaps our most grievous fault lies in committing in a manipulative sort of way. We commit not as *givers* but rather as *takers*—though we are often clever at concealing our intention.

Two biblical ideals guide us in our commitments with others.

First, as Christians, our commitment to others must involve generous doses of *submission*. Peter talks about *not* repaying evil for evil, and *not* snapping back at those who say unkind things. Rather, we must try to live at peace "even if (we) must run after it to catch and hold it" (1 Peter 3:11, TLB).

Such commitment leaves us vulnerable to abuse. This is acknowledged by the apostle. But hear his response: "Usually no one will hurt you for wanting to do good. But even if they should, you are to be envied, for God will reward you for it. Quietly trust yourself to Christ your Lord" (vv. 13-15, TLB).

Then, meditate on this final tag line: "Remember, if God wants you to suffer, it is better to suffer for doing good than for doing wrong!" (v. 17, TLB)

Submission must be seen for what it is: a win-win situation.[11]

The principle of submission, though biblical, works in athletics. Paul "Bear" Bryant rose from being an Arkansas plowman, to become the "winningest" coach in the history of U.S. college football. Listen to his secret:

> I have learned how to hold a team together. How to lift some men up, how to calm down others, until finally

---

10. Lewis B. Smedes, op. cit., p. 77.
11. Submission means "voluntarily cooperating with anyone out of love and respect for God [and] for that person." Submitting to nonbelievers is difficult, but is vital to leading them to Jesus—though we're never called to disobey God. Submission has these four dimensions:
- functional—distinguishing our roles and the work we do;
- relational—loving acknowledgment of another's value;
- reciprocal—mutual, humble cooperation with another;
- universal—acknowledgment by the church of the all-encompassing lordship of Jesus.
Life Application Bible, op. cit., p. 620.

they've got one heartbeat together, a team. There's just three things I'd ever say:

If anything goes bad, *I* did it.
If anything goes semi-good, then *we* did it.
If anything goes real good, then *they* did it.[12]

Giving credit to others. Accepting blame. Not insisting on rights. Never seeking revenge. That's what God's Word means by submission.

One final suggestion. Our commitment to others must include doling out a surplus of *encouragement*. As we stated elsewhere, the term implies infusing another with courage.

The fifth chapter of 1 Thessalonians has much to say about this imperative (vv. 11-23). Consider this a "checklist for encouragers":

Verse	Example	Suggested application
11	Build each other up.	Point out to someone a quality you appreciate in them.
12	Give honor to leaders.	Look for ways to cooperate.
13	Think highly of leaders.	Withold your next critical comment.
13	Give wholehearted love.	Say "thank you" to leaders for their efforts.
13	Avoid quarreling.	Search for ways to get along.
14	Warn the lazy.	Challenge someone to join you in a project.
14	Comfort the frightened.	Remind them of God's promises.
14	Care for the weak.	Love and pray for them.
14	Practice patience.	Recall situations that try your patience, then plan ahead how you will stay calm.
15	Resist revenge.	"Kill" enemies with kindness.

12. Ted W. Engstrom, op. cit. p. 112.

16	Be joyful.	In the midst of turmoil, remember that God is in control.
17	Pray continuously.	God is always with you—talk to Him.
18	Be thankful.	Make a list of God's gifts; thank Him for each one.[13]

Submission. Encouragement. Let's commit ourselves to ministering to others by obeying these biblical admonitions. They require great courage on our part. But we can be assured of this: God is eager to provide an ample supply!

There is, however, one more kind of commitment. It is essential, though often slighted. Let's focus on it now.

Commitment to Principles, Our Means of Obedience

In our day, we seem to be obsessed with finding a low-demand Gospel. One that's guaranteed to never inconvenience nor produce burdensome convictions. And why not? Everything from soft drinks to peaches seems to be going "lite!"

With a serious point to make with his humor, Eutychus contrasts "heavy" and "light" religion in these manners:

Heavy	Light
bulky black Bibles with words of Jesus in red;	a version that translates Nebuchadnezzar, Zerubbabel, and Jezebel as Waylon, Willie, and Dolly;
knowing doctrines like the Atonement and Redemption;	simplifies systematic theology into a triune formula: KNOW *yourself,* LOVE *yourself,* BE *yourself;*
a day of fasting;	skipping breakfast when you're in a hurry, or grabbing a salad bar lunch instead of your usual Whopper;

---

13. *Life Application Bible,* op. cit., p. 538.

| an all-night prayer vigil; | a few minutes of prayer and share; |
| Seven Deadly Sins; | Seven Minutes with God.[14] |

His conclusion: "On second thought, perhaps we don't need to lighten the gospel. Maybe we just need to digest the one we've got."[15]

R.V.G. Tasker, former New Testament professor at the University of London, pulls no punches when he declares:

As disciples [we] are called to be a moral disinfectant in a world where moral standards are low, constantly changing or non-existent.[16]

That means one thing: We must not opt for a "lite" Gospel. Rather, we are called to an uncompromised obedience to biblical principles.

Unfortunately, many of us seem preoccupied with this question: How close can we come to this world's sordid values and still be a Christian? With such an attitude, we're apt to fall prey to the demons of humanism, secularism, intellectualism, and materialism. The result? Eventually our faith is severely diluted—or completely evaporated.

What must we do? God's Word is adamant in proclaiming that we must respond in two ways.

First, we must take protective measures. Let's not kid ourselves; Satan "prowls around like a roaring lion looking for someone to devour" (1 Peter 5:8).

Furthermore, sin is an ever-present, subtle temptation that is regressive in its nature. The first Psalm spells out the steps of that regression: "Blessed is the man who does not *walk* in the council of the wicked or *stand* in the way of sinners or *sit*

---

14. *Christianity Today,* September 21, 1984, Volume 28, Number 13, "Eutychus and His Kin," p. 6. (Eutychus is a pseudonym.)
15. Ibid.
16. Charles R. Swindoll, *Improving Your Serve* (Waco, Texas: Word, 1981), pp. 132-133.

in the seat of mockers" (Ps. 1:1-2).

Allow me to interpret. When we stop "run(ning) the race with perseverance" (with our eyes on Jesus), our hearts begin to gravitate toward evil (Heb. 12:1-2). At first we walk—and catch a closer look at sin's enticements. Soon, we're likely to stand in sin's environment—longing to become full participants. Finally, we take our seat among those who relish sinful living.

And it all occurs so rapidly. Just like riding a descending escalator.

What does this imply? Plain and simple, it means that we must avoid participation in evil activities, in questionable environments, with sinful persons. To not do so is to invite entrapment.

Paul puts it in these emphatic words: "Therefore come out from among them and be separate, says the Lord. Touch no unclean thing, and I will receive you"(2 Cor. 6:17).

There should be no slowing down to have a better look or to touch. We must keep sprinting for the "prize"!

Something seems to be occurring among many believers that concerns me greatly. As they attempt to attract and be attractive to sinners "in order to lure them into the church," believers are becoming full participants in the sinners' value systems and lifestyles.[17]

It is plain to see that the secular world has become their model. For example, their religious music reflects the world's beat—and is presented with Hollywood choreography. Theology is made to sound more like contemporary psychology. Standards of behavior and ethics are loosened and eventually ignored.

The idea of these Christians is to stand for little (or for most everything the world stands for) so that outsiders feel less alienated.

At best, their approach is wimpish. At worst, it is downright deceptive. That is, unless these people really no longer stand

---

17. See Jon Johnston, *Will Evangelicalism Survive Its Own Popularity?* (Grand Rapids: Zondervan, 1980).

for much of anything. In that case, unfortunately, they're being sincere.

The truth is this: We must stand for biblical principles, which are fleshed out in personal convictions. These kinds of personal convictions may make us seem a little different to some people—though in ways not intended to either impress or offend.

What are your convictions? Allow me to share a few of mine, most of which, I feel, are grounded as much in social scientific rationale as in biblical principle.

1. I deeply resent the name of God being used in a casual or disrespectful manner. His Name is too wonderful to be taken in vain. [18]
2. I consider all forms of gambling—from grocery store lottery to Vegas slot machines—to be an affront to our Heavenly Father. [19]

---

18. It has been said that a person's name is his most valuable possession. In biblical times, persons were given names that implied specific traits. When they changed, frequently their names were changed (e.g., Saul became Paul). God's name and nature are synonymous. (See Ps. 8:1.) That's why His name is to be hallowed and revered. Jews even refused to pronounce His name. Today, we not only say His name, but we often do so in an irreverent manner. Each time we do, we are, in effect, insulting His Person.

19. Social scientists have researched the maladies that result from gambling. Certain weaker personality types succumb to irrationality. The poor, groping for instant wealth, are drawn in to the extent of giving up necessities to participate. Few gain, except for the criminal elements. Nevertheless, gambling is seizing our nation's affections. (The University of Nevada, Reno, even offers a minor in the subject!) Basically, the underlying premise of gambling is this: We can win more than we contribute, though always at the expense of others who participate (i.e., getting something for nothing). Such thinking does not square with New Testament teaching nor with what is best for our society.

Valerie C. Lorenz, executive director of the National Center for Pathological Gambling Inc. in Baltimore, recently stated that at least 3 percent of America's adult population are "compulsive gamblers." They are "willing to risk home, family, job, integrity, or health for it." She maintains that bingo games and state lotteries are the nurseries for compulsive gamblers. The great expansion of the latter gives her, and should give us, great concern.

(USA Today, August 28, 1989, p. 11A.) The same newspaper issue offers this "USA Snapshot," which profiles the typical "compulsive gambler": owes $43,158; is 39.8 years old; was 13 when made first bet; 83 percent completed high school; 25 percent completed college (Ibid. p. 1A).

Ready for a couple more? Here goes:

3. I feel that you always "lose with booze." Given the effects of alcohol in our society, I believe Christians should completely refrain.[20]
4. I maintain that an uncompromising stand must be taken against pornography—whether it appears on the printed page or on the cinema or television screen.[21]
5. I deeply resent racial slurs, even in jest. Our national track record is too pathetic to indulge in such innuendos.

Except for those behaviors expressly stated (by word or principle) in Scripture, I would not expect all of us to agree with my convictions. And that's as it should be, for convictions are tailor-made to our individual walk with Christ.

20. Alcoholic beverages wreak more havoc than, perhaps, any other facet of our culture. Over two thirds of our homicides, divorces, automobile accidents, and suicides are related to drinking. Some would say, "We can learn to drink responsibly, like they do in Europe." Where in Europe? France has double our alcoholism rate, and a full 25 percent in Holland are full-scale alcoholics. Some would say, "The Bible does not explicitly prohibit drinking—though it condemns drunkenness." My response: "Neither does the Bible condemn heroin." God's Word gives us timeless principles to apply to our times. Today, unlike in biblical times, alcoholism is a social problem of grave dimensions. In addition, our drinks are 10-20 times more potent than in Bible times. Question: Would we keep a dog that bit 20 percent of all the people who entered our home? Not likely. Yet we drink socially, when we know that over 20 percent of all "social drinkers" become problem drinkers. It doesn't figure—especially for Christians.
21. Regarding *printed matter,* it is encouraging that Christians have recently boycotted stores that sell sexually explicit periodicals. As a result, some of these materials have been removed from shelves.

It is no secret that *movies* today are saturated with pornographic scenes—even those rated "PG" (Parental Guidance Suggested). It really all comes down to how we choose to expend our money, time, and energy. And what we choose symbolizes our values—to God, to others, to ourselves. With this in mind, avoiding pornographically prone environments seems to be a wise course of action.

This in no way lets *television* off the hook. Donald Wildmon, head of the Christian Leaders for Responsible Television, has 3,000 volunteers monitoring the networks—and threatens to boycott products that sponsor unfit shows. (In a May 1989 telephone survey by Oxtoby-Smity, over half of those polled stated that they were "bothered a lot" by television programming. Most distasteful were violence, sex, profanity, and insults to women. See *Family Circle,* October 17, 1989.)

The key issue is *not* so much whether certain convictions are right; rather, it's whether we have adopted *any* for ourselves. Have we committed ourselves to doing, or refraining from doing, certain things in order to live closer to Christ?

Please understand, I'm certainly not advocating any salvation by works. The "holier than thou" mentality is a turn-off to God and others.

Nevertheless, He does measure our love, in part, by our obedience. (See John 15:10, 14.) One key way we obey is by accepting certain convictions—as His Spirit and His Word sensitize our minds and hearts.

Question: Are there guidelines to follow in choosing certain courses of action? Yes. Absolutely. I have found it extremely helpful to ask these nine questions, taken from the Book of 1 Corinthians:

- Does it help my witness for Christ? (9:19-22)
- Am I motivated by a desire to help others know Christ? (9:23)
- Does it help me do my best? (9:25)
- Is it against a specific command in Scripture, and thus, sin? (10:12)
- Is it best and helpful? (10:23, 33)
- Am I thinking only of myself, or do I truly care about the other people involved? (10:24)
- Am I acting lovingly or selfishly? (10:28-31)
- Does it glorify God? (10:31)
- Will it encourage someone else to sin? (10:32)[22]

It all really comes down to choices of commitment. Which activities deserve our time, money, and energy priorities? We all need to honestly respond to this pivotal issue on a daily basis.

There is a second way we must respond to biblical principles. *Since we're involved in a battle, we must be more than protective—we must become assertive.*

To refrain from sin is commendable, but we must also challenge evil. Take the initiative. Go on the offensive. Just as our

---

22. *Life Application Bible*, op. cit., p. 436.

Lord did when He faced up to the lynch mob that attempted to annihilate the adulterous woman, or the money changers who tried to desecrate His Father's temple.

We must emerge from our tidy and smug religious cocoons to take important stands. Many of us are. The rest of us must do more than applaud, we must join in.

The anti-abortion and anti-pornography efforts have received the most publicity. But other critical battles must be waged, such as:

- boycotting products, whose companies prey on the helpless in Third World countries—their people, their resources.
- responding to AIDS victims in a loving, nonjudgmental manner—and challenging other Christians to do likewise.
- actively campaigning for qualified candidates who share our biblical perspective.
- following our Lord's example, by joining in the battle to defend the powerless and victimized—the aged, imprisoned, orphaned, famished.

We need not look far to find causes that are near to the heart of God. Where the forces of evil and good are engaged. And once we locate the battlefield, we must not be timid about—as the hymn says—joining in the "battle for truth."

It's time to begin playing march music, readying our weapons, getting a good reading on the enemy, and—most of all— allowing Him to fill us with His courage.

Grasp the imagery in this command in Ephesians:

Finally, be strong in the Lord and in His mighty power. Put on the full armor of God so you can take your stand against the devil's schemes. For our struggle is not against flesh and blood, but against the rulers, against the authorities, against the powers of this dark world and against the spiritual forces of evil in the heavenly realms (Eph. 6:10-12).

A couple of facts should be disclosed about our spiritual

warfare. First, the battle is not easy. Second, it demands that we not become too entrenched in affairs of this world. Paul says: "Endure hardship . . . like a good soldier of Christ Jesus. No one serving as a soldier gets involved in civilian affairs—he wants to please his commanding officer" (2 Tim. 2:3-4).

Be assured, however, that the victory is well worth the sacrifice. It is really His battle. And as strange as it may seem, it is already won!

Guard Dogs, Graffiti, and True Grit

Son of a coal miner in a family of eight—without the privileges of education. This describes a man who went on to minister for 48 years. The last 23 years of his life, from age 54 to 77, were spent deep in the inner city of Los Angeles. I never knew a more committed Christian. He loved Jesus so much that I've seen the very mention of His name bring tears to this man's eyes. As for his parishioners and community, he loved them. He cared for their sick, counseled their troubled, and cautioned their sinful.

One night he came home without his socks. He had given them to a drifter whose feet were cold.

I recall his picketing against the gambling casinos, which were threatening to invade the city. He knew that anguish would follow.

His earthly payoff? He was repeatedly assaulted. His house was robbed. His church was vandalized so many times that he had a guard dog on the premises. How ironic—a dog guarding the house of God!

Toward the end of his ministry, the city cited him as "Man of the Year." He was made official chaplain of his town. He seemed unimpressed, for he looked forward to a far greater and more lasting reward.

This faithful servant "retired," to spend his last two years establishing a ministry in nursing homes. One day, with sadness in his eyes, he said to me, "I heard that they bulldozed my little church. They couldn't find anyone willing to become the pastor." My heart suffered with his.

Then it happened. One day he slumped in his chair with a

stroke. They took him to the hospital—with a delirious mind and confused speech.

But somehow His love for Jesus was so ingrained in his inner being, that he repeated these words to the doctors: "Praise the Lord." Then, to their amazement, he began to softly sing, "We Shall Overcome."

Next to Jesus, this man has influenced my life more than any other. I saw his faithfulness without applause, his obedience without earthly reward, his courage without much acclaim.

Perfect? Far from it. A saint? He'd be very uncomfortable being called one. I think I did hear him refer to himself as a beggar, who went about telling other beggars where to find bread. The Bread of Life.

I had the privilege of tasting some of that bread! You see, that man was my father. His commitment to the principles of courage provides an excellent example of what it means to stand strong in the face of fear.

CHAPTER TWELVE

Hound Dogs and Other Suckers: Courage Is Loyalty

Buddy: "What could be worse than unanswered questions?"
Mensch: "Unquestioned answers." (Mensch comic strip)

"Genius is the infinite capacity for taking life by the scruff of the neck." (Christopher Quill)

As with birds and insects, God designs our wings to match our weights. His help is sufficient for our burdens. (Robert Schuller)

Some time ago, I read a true story by Suhail Hanna that I can still hardly comprehend. Let me share it.

World War II was at its height. Forces were engaged in what was known as, "The Battle of the Bulge"—or "The Christmas War of 1944." The fighting was fierce in the bitter cold and snow.

The Allied Forces bombed and established control of a strategic area. The commanding officer turned to several of his men and said, "Sweep across that field, and kill all German soldiers still entrenched in the snow. I want no prisoners. Absolutely none!"

One of the American soldiers selected gives his account of what happened next. "As I walked, I immediately shot and killed two wounded and suffering soldiers." He continues, "Then, suddenly I approached a tall, young guy with a broad Teutonic forehead.

"He was leaning against a tree. He wasn't wounded—simply exhausted. He had no food, no water, no comrades in sight, no ammunition. Fear, fatigue, defeat, and loneliness overwhelmed him. He spoke English with a beautiful vonderful-vorld-type accent.

"When I noticed a little black Bible in his shirt pocket," he reminisces, "we started to talk about Jesus and salvation.

"Wouldn't you know it, that lanky German soldier turned out to be a born-again Christian who deeply loved the Lord.

"I gave him water from my canteen; I even gave him crackers. Then, we prayed and read God's Word together. And we wept together too."

His voice began to tremble, as tears splashed down his cheeks. His face began to reflect anguish.

"It seems like only yesterday. We stood a foot or so apart, as he read a Psalm from his German Bible. Then, I read Romans 12 from my *King James* translation. He showed me a black-and-white picture of his wife and daughter."

The soldier took a deep breath. "You see, in those days, I was a young man in my early twenties. I had just graduated from a Christian college in Illinois and hadn't had time to sort out my thoughts on the war.

"Maybe that's why I did what I did.

"I bid my German brother farewell, took several steps away, then returned to the soldier. Romans 13, the 'thou shalt not kill' commandment, the promises of eternal life, the Prince of Peace, the Sunday school distinction between killing and murder, the irrationality of war—all swirled in my mind.

"When the German soldier saw me returning, he bowed his head and closed his eyes in that classic prayer posture.

"Then it happened. I said three crisp sentences that I still repeat once or twice a week when I have nightmares about the war, 'You're a Christian. I am too. See you later.'

"In less than a second, I transformed that defenseless Christian soldier into a corpse."[1]

The Bland Following the Blind

No doubt, the young American feared disobeying the orders of his superior. That could have gotten him court marshaled. And disgraced back home.

Besides, Christian or no Christian, this German soldier was part of the German war machine—which was attempting to overtake the world.

The American had to follow orders. His commanding officer always knew best. That's what he had been told since boot camp. But inside his heart of hearts, he knew what he had done was wrong. His "heavenly Commander" did *not* approve.

His loyalty had been a *blind loyalty*. A robotic reflex. A complete disregard for his conscience and better judgment.[2]

Is blind loyalty commendable? Perhaps it is for hound dogs—who learn unquestioned obedience, even if it means giving their lives to divert the attention of a 500-pound grizzly bear. But what about people? Should we manifest hound-dog loyalty? Not really, because it allows others to do our thinking and to determine our fate. Then we're forced to live with the nightmarish consequences, and to absorb the guilt.

If you don't believe me, ask Chuck Colson, whose blind loyalty to President Richard Nixon caused him to break the law.

Travel with me to Japan. Let's examine the testimony of the general who ordered that country's attack on Pearl Harbor. Why did he do it? Blind loyalty.

At a Youth for Christ rally, I once heard this former leader of the Emperor's navy describe the inner turmoil that took place in his heart. Soon after the war, he repented and became a victorious Christian. His underlying message: Blind loyalty isn't enough. Not by a long shot.

---

1. Suhail Hanna, "Piecemeal Peace," *Eternity*, December 1981, p. 30.
2. See chapter 7, page 89, which reveals Kohlberg's morality model. It is apparent that "blind faith" corresponds to stage 4, "Law and Order." Recall that Kohlberg states that few rise above this stage.

Essentially, the word "loyalty" means "being faithful to one's allegiance or oath."[3] Loyalty comes in two major forms:

- loyalty that is *imposed on us from another or others* (blind loyalty);
- loyalty that *we impose upon ourselves,* because of principles we accept as true and trustworthy (convinced loyalty).

Christian courage has little in common with the first of these. However, the second is the natural outgrowth of Christian courage.

Open Eyes, Open Mind, Open Heart

Does our Saviour want our loyalty? Absolutely.

But only after we have weighed the facts and are convinced in our own minds. Why? Because He wants us to fully understand the cost involved.

Jesus spells out His price in these words, "Anyone who wants to be My follower must love Me far more than he does his own father, mother, wife, children, brothers, or sisters—yes, more than his own life—otherwise he cannot be my disciple" (Luke 14:26, TLB).

Then He adds, "And anyone who does not carry his cross and follow me cannot be my disciple" (v. 27).

That is something to really think about! It's quite a price to pay. Here is a kind of loyalty that demands great courage. Thus, our decision must not be impulsive; it must be very deliberate, and methodically reasoned out.

Jesus says so. After specifying the cost, He recommends carefully weighing the consequences. Like the man who builds a tower. "Will he not first sit down and estimate the cost to see if he has enough money to complete it?" Or like a king going to war. "Will he not first sit down and consider whether he is able with ten thousand to oppose the one coming against him with twenty thousand?" (vv. 28-33)

The point we've established is this: Unlike many cult leaders

---

3. "Loyalty," *The Random House Dictionary,* Jess Stein, ed. (New York: Ballantine Books, 1980), p. 534.

we've heard about, Jesus doesn't want us to be blindly loyal to Him. Rather, He wants us to be so convinced that *His* way is *our* way, that we'll be eager to take courageous stands. Without that strong inner assurance, we're likely to "flake out in the stretch."

The truth stands: Just because we decide, on our own, whom (or what) we'll be loyal to, that certainly doesn't guarantee that our choices will be wise.

Fool's Gold

Many of us are sorely tempted to give primary allegiance to items of lesser value. Like miners during the days of the California Gold Rush, we are deceived by a kind of "fool's gold." It *looks* authentic—but in reality, it's worth nothing.

What are some kinds of fool's gold that many of us grasp for?

1. Job—For most of us males, our occupations assume top priority. Jobs can be the main basis for our identities and the primary focus of our attention. We're fiercely loyal to bosses and faithful to our jobs' requirements. I know of one workaholic who has lost his wife, children, and his sanity.

2. Family—As the preceding words of Jesus spell out, our biological kin must be subordinate to our relationship with God. On several occasions, He had to explain this to Mary and His brothers. Renowned missionary, E. Stanley Jones, had to pry himself away from his aged, demanding mother in order to follow God's leading to India. Though close-knit families are a worthy goal, we need to be cautious about allowing them to dominate our loyalties.

3. Money—Thoughts of mammon can consume us. Charles Swindoll tells about a West Palm Beach woman who died of malnutrition after wasting away to 50 pounds. Investigators found that she lived in a veritable pigpen. She had begged food from neighbors and gone to the Salvation Army for clothes. Amid her belongings, two keys were found to safe-deposit boxes. The first revealed 700 AT&T stock certificates, as well as hundreds of securities, bonds, and other valuable certificates—plus $200,000 in cash. The second box contained

$600,000! This woman was a millionaire who died a stark victim of starvation in a humble hovel. To paraphrase another, *She knew the worth of everything, but the value of nothing.*[4]

To these three forms of fool's gold can be added many others: friends, home, cars, celebrities, nature, hobbies, service clubs, sports, and food, to name just a few.

In summary, loyalty is something that should be our choice. Jesus tells us to cautiously weigh options, and make our own decisions. But in choosing, it is imperative that we establish priorities according to His scheme of things.

That means choosing Him, His concerns, His commandments, and His will first. We must be absolutely loyal to these. Though few of us really do this, I'm quite certain that most of us agree on its rightness. But from that point on, the loyalty business can get pretty sticky. Let me offer a brief testimonial.

Searching for My Crowd

Don't get me wrong; I'm a *joiner* like many of the rest of us. I belong to a denomination, professional organizations, the Sheraton Club, and —oh yes, I almost forgot—I'm a rabid Dodger fan!

The certificates of these organizations are on my walls, on cards in my wallet, and even inscribed on clothes I wear. (Though some seasons, I've seriously considered wearing my Dodger jacket inside out!)

Yet on second thought, I guess I really don't "belong"—in the sense that I bury my identity in most of these organizations. That's because some time ago I bought into the belief that only Jesus can control my life without destroying it.

If He is, in actuality, the only One who controls me—if He possesses my primary loyalty—then I don't feel right in allowing myself to be "swallowed up" by any man-made social body. That's good in a way, because I've never found any one group that I totally agree with. There are always a few places where

---

4. Charles R. Swindoll, *Improving Your Serve: The Art of Unselfish Living* (Waco, Texas: Word Books, 1981), p. 50.

my identity, and the identity of the group, simply don't mesh.

Here's a bird's-eye view of my situation. Though far from being fanatical, I'm fairly conservative in my theology—holding to the absolute authority of God's Word, the divinity of Christ, and even to some personal convictions. But, when I talk with other persons who are theologically conservative, I invariably pick up on "redneck" talk. These kinds of "loose cannon" comments are made:

- "We should line up all people with AIDS and shoot them."
- "If anyone came after my gun, I'd blow them away."
- "All people on welfare are chiselers."
- "We should feed the homeless to the starving in Bangladesh."

These statements are often topped off with an ethnic joke or two.

I instantly recognize that I can't identify with these people either. Go ahead, color Jon Johnston "liberal," when it comes to nonviolence and believing that we should render compassion.

So in reality I guess I'm a hybrid. A conservative liberal. Or, if you prefer, a liberal conservative. Not really at home in either camp.

When I'm tempted to second-guess my stance, which to many may seem inconsistent and counterproductive, I think about some courageous heroes—who just happen to share my basic position. Persons like John Wesley, Chuck Colson, Mother Teresa, Tony Campolo, Senator Mark Hatfield.

And that picks me up better than drinking iced tea.

All of this is to say, that our loyalty to organizations must be subordinate to our loyalty to biblical principles. To the extent we're convinced that organizations square with these positions, they merit our loyalty. To the degree they deviate, no matter how worthy they are perceived to be, we should resign from their team.

Taking this kind of position requires a heavy dose of courage—courage that can only come from being inhabited by the very presence of God's Spirit. Why is this so? Because our natural inclinations pull us in the *opposite* direction.

All Tarred with the Same Brush

Calvin Redekop has written a fine book, entitled *The Free Church and Seductive Culture*. In it he presents four sociological principles that push all of us in the direction of becoming indiscriminate loyalists.

1. Ethnocentrism principle—We defend, boost, and identify ourselves with the groups to which we belong. We see things from their perspective. (Contrast a southern Alabama KKK member's perspective, with that of a New England ACLU member.)

2. Socialization principle—We become like persons in our social system. They are our reference group. We continuously compare and contrast ourselves with them. In short, they determine the values, beliefs, and norms that we internalize. (Notice how teenagers seem to talk and dress alike, and how they "tolerate" the same music!)

3. Reciprocity principle—We usually don't give something away without receiving something of equal value. Our social networks supply us with power, status, and prestige. We resist the inevitable withdrawal pains that are associated with relinquishing these. Thus, we're likely to remain cemented in our present relationships. (I know someone who despises his church, yet, wouldn't think of attending another. He has "too much to lose.")

4. Self-deceiving principle—We have an uncanny ability to misinterpret and pervert objective reality. We "see" what we want to see. Our rose-colored glasses show us a fantasized reality. Thus, many of us are unable to perceive our organizational structures clearly—or judge them objectively.[5] (I once knew someone who was so cantankerous, that the only good thing you could say about him was that he wasn't born a twin! Yet, to his mother, he was angelic. *That's* a lack of objectivity.)

To simplify and abbreviate these important principles, we do plenty of mindless flag-waving, conforming, reward-hoarding

---

5. Calvin Redekop, *The Free Church and Seductive Culture* (Philadelphia, Pa.: Herald Press, 1970), pp. 84-86.

and rationalizing. Together, these inhibit us from seeing our social involvements as they really are. And they keep us from being willing to refuse them our loyalty.

As Christians, we must not allow our roots to dig down too deeply in organizational structures—whether they be associated with church, family, job, or recreation. Furthermore, we must, constantly, judge how closely their goals and activities correspond with the teachings in God's Word.

Here's where courage enters the picture. If we detect incongruities between our social networks and His standards, we must "bite the bullet" and back off from (or find new) social networks.

Is it okay to be loyal to organizations? Sure. Once we're sure they will help, rather than hinder, our walk with God.

A certain amount of loyalty is expected, and even demanded, by the associations we join. In fact, they need it if they are to survive. But, like crabgrass and fingernails, our loyalty must be periodically examined and trimmed back. Otherwise, it's bound to get out of hand.

All Our "Loyalty Eggs" in One Basket

From the foregoing discussion, this author contends that loyalty to biblical principles is essential. And that implies one conclusion: Our ultimate loyalty must be to Jesus Christ, the Living Word. All other loyalties must be subordinated to (and judged by) that one pivotal loyalty.

Doing that requires a mature spiritual courage—a courage that can only come by relying on His omnipotent power. And that means "losing ourselves in Him."

What do we have to gain by submerging our identities in His? So that His purposes become ours? And that His battles also become ours?

The Bible proclaims these rich dividends:

Rom. 3:24   We are declared "not guilty" of sin.
Rom. 8:1   No condemnation awaits us.
Rom. 8:2   We are free from the vicious cycle of sin and death.

1 Cor. 1:2	We are acceptable to God through Jesus Christ.
1 Cor. 1:30	We are pure and holy.
1 Cor. 15:22	We will rise again.
2 Cor. 3:17	We are free from trying to be saved by being good.
2 Cor. 5:17	We are brand new people inside.
2 Cor. 5:21	We are full of God's goodness.
Gal. 3:28	We are one in Christ with all other believers.
Eph. 1:3	We are blessed with every spiritual blessing.
Eph. 1:4	We are holy, faultless, and covered with God's love.
Eph. 1:5-6	We belong to Christ.
Eph. 1:7	Our sins are taken away and we are forgiven.
Eph. 1:10-11	We will live with Christ forever; we are gifts to God.
Eph. 1:13	We are marked as belonging to God by the Holy Spirit.
Eph. 2:6	We have been lifted from the grave to sit with Christ in glory.
Eph. 2:10	We have been given new lives.
Eph. 2:13	We have been brought near to God.
Eph. 3:6	We will receive great blessings.
Eph. 3:12	We can come fearlessly into God's presence.
Eph. 5:29-30	We are part of Christ's body, the church.
Col. 2:10	We have everything because we have Christ; we are filled with God.
Col. 2:11	We are set free from our evil desires.
2 Tim. 2:10	We will have eternal glory.[6]

---

6. *Life Application Bible: New Testament,* Bruce B. Barton, ed. (Wheaton, Ill.: Tyndale House Publishers, Inc. and Youth for Christ/USA, 1987), p. 493.

Who could ask for anything more? The past is forgiven. The present is meaningful and significant. The future assured. Great payoffs! But best of all, by identifying with Him, we buy into rich, continuous, fellowship with Him. And there's no better company—anywhere!

Perhaps it is under conditions of persecution that we achieve our closest intimacy with, and greatest loyalty to, the Saviour. One man convinced me of this. Here is his courageous story.

Twenty Mongolian Winters

On a recent trip to China I met a true hero. This man was asked to recant his faith shortly after the Communist Revolution, and he emphatically refused.

That earned him a life sentence in a Mongolian prison.

After nearly twenty-one years, at age 65, he was released and put under house arrest in Beijing. Someone put us in contact, and I had the rare opportunity to converse with him about those years of incarceration.

He smiled as he thanked God for helping him to persevere. And for his recent release—which was totally unexpected. He also rejoiced in the converts he had made in the prison. As I remember, some of those converts even included the guards.

His face grimaced, though, as he spoke of the extreme hardship that he had to endure. It was beyond belief. Many of his fellow prisoners couldn't take the abuse and died. But he was somehow able to endure.

I asked that he might offer a word of prayer. His words were electric. His spirit was contagious. His devotion seemed so deep. It was like being in the presence of an Old Testament prophet.

After we prayed, I looked at him and naively said, "I can hardly imagine what you went through. You were literally tortured beyond belief."

Without batting an eye, or giving the slightest hint of self-pity, he looked at me and said, *"What I endured was nothing compared to the Crucifixion."*

Here is a man that so closely identified with our Lord and

His sufferings, that he purposely compared his ordeal with that of His Master. As a result of his intense loyalty, he simply refused to look back on his extreme trial with bitterness or resentment—or even regret.

Instead, there was a bright note of thanksgiving. Thanksgiving for the privilege of sharing in Christ's sufferings (cf. 1 Peter 4:13). Thanksgiving for his "premature" release—for he had resigned himself to dying there in prison.

With a broad smile, he looked at me and joked, "See here (pointing to his dark head of hair), God didn't even let my hair go gray!"

For this man, and for all of us who follow Jesus, courage is indeed loyalty. Loyalty to Him and to all He stands for.

And when the cost is weighed against His eternal dividends, we realize that it is a minimal price to pay. Even if it must be paid in a Mongolian prison.

Try something. I have, and it has provided a tremendous uplift. The next time your problems seem overwhelming— which could be today—just pause long enough to bow your head and pray these words: *"Dear Lord, what I am enduring is really nothing, compared to Your Crucifixion."*

A PARTING WORD

I had to smile when I recently encountered this sign:

> Lost dog:
> 3 legs,
> blind in left eye,
> missing right ear,
> tail broken,
> accidently neutered.
> *Answers to name of "Lucky"*[1]

Many of us answer to the name of "courageous." We relish it when others perceive us in this way. And we like to think of ourselves as stalwarts: indomitable, unyielding, unconquerable. Real giant killers!

Why do we want to claim the name *courageous?* Because from our cradles onward, we've learned that courage is a universally acclaimed virtue. It is a badge worn proudly—a virtue that nations, communities, families, and coaches handsomely reward. Something that could, very likely, get us in the Hall of Fame, *Who's Who,* the *Guinness Book of World Records,* or even a history book.

But unfortunately, often our actual characteristics fail to square with our courage tag. We're considered courageous, but in reality it's a clear case of mistaken identity!

We know it, because the evidence is indisputable.

We wince, or hide, when faced with a challenge. We're obsessed with our comfort. We duck anything that makes us fearful in the slightest degree. We're so paranoid that even our fears have fears!

---

1. Sign located on wall of J.C. Plumbing store in Thousand Oaks, Calif. Source unknown.

167

In short, we've calculated the cost of true courage, and we're unwilling to pay it.

Please Step to the Cashier

This book maintains that authentic courage is, indeed, costly— in all of the forms we've described. It's not something that can be quickly picked up at some bargain basement. It can't be learned by a "three-step formula" at some weekend seminar, or even acquired from courageous parents.

In a way, becoming courageous is a lot like mastering the violin. I'm reminded of the lady who rushed up to famed violinist Fritz Kreisler after a concert and said, "I'd give my life to play as beautifully as you do."

Kreisler softly replied: "Ma'am, I did."

Courage requires a lifetime of arduous dedication.

Question: What are we dedicating our lives to? Security? The purchase and maintenance of expensive "toys"? Avoidance of conflict? Safety? Presenting a facade to others? Dousing our fears?

Or, by contrast, are our sights fixed on righting wrongs, correcting injustices, shouldering unpopular but worthy causes, or keeping our chins up in the face of the harshest adversities? And all without resentment or regret?

Even these are insufficient from our Christian perspective. Scores of devout humanists, atheists, and secularists sacrificially champion noble causes. And in their eyes, this makes them self-sufficient and even self-righteous. They claim to be better than the average Christian.

Then what, essentially, is unique about Christian courage?

First, the source *of Christian courage is God.* A favorite verse of mine is, "For God did not give us a spirit of timidity, but of power, of love and of self-discipline" (2 Tim. 1:7).

We don't have to work up our nerve—or generate enough willpower to be courageous.

Rather, Christ entreats us to relinquish our timidity and fear to His care (1 Peter 5:7), and open our hearts to receive the inner strength that He generously provides. How does this come about? Through fervent and sincere prayer—prayer that causes us to look up in faith and expectancy.

Again, for us it's not by effort but by surrender that we receive our courage. And the supply is always generous.

Second, the focus *of Christian courage is found in His reliable Word.* It is here where we find those critical issues and attitudes that demand our action. With assurance Paul says, *"All Scripture is God-breathed and is useful for teaching, rebuking, correcting and training in righteousness, so that the man of God may be thoroughly equipped for every good work" (2 Tim. 3:16).*

Third, the motivator *of courage is prayer.* An old adage goes: Satan flees when he sees the weakest of us on our knees. Why? Because he knows that we are on our way to becoming bold.

Prayer linkage with God means that our timidity will evaporate, and His promises will become our possessions.

To paraphrase my respected friend, Eugene Stowe: prayer does for us what a tuning fork does for a piano. It eliminates discord between us and God, so that we're on the right spiritual pitch. And the removal of such discord prompts us to be courageous.[2]

Shrinking Supply, Expanding Demand

As previously stated, courage is more rare than it is plentiful. And many of us believe its supply resembles the world's crude oil supply; it is rapidly diminishing. That is truly tragic—at a time when challenges seem to be growing in number and complexity.

Even a passing glance at what is predicted for the twenty-first century sends chills up our spine: Acute food and energy shortages. Overpopulation. More sophisticated drugs—and their possible legalization. A worldwide AIDS epidemic that could rival the Black Plague.

Furthermore, in those pockets where our courage is found,

---

2. Stated by Eugene Stowe, Chairman of the Board of General Superintendents, Church of the Nazarene, at the Anaheim District Retreat, November 1989.

it seems to mostly take the form of maximizing our self-interest. It takes the form of getting our way, so that we're one up on situations or persons. Or insisting on our rights. Or pushing our way to acquire increased power, privilege, prestige, possessions. In short, it takes the form of taking care of number one!

Christian courage, by contrast, is directed toward *obeying* God's Word and serving others. It is directed toward giving rather than getting and toward holiness rather than personal happiness.

How is this possible? Again, the presence of His Spirit within our hearts gently pulls us in this direction—if we're totally dependent on Him.

Even when suffering is required—as it often is—we will not flinch. At least, not for long. Why? Because we know that we *"share in His (Christ's) sufferings in order that we may also share in His glory"* (Rom. 8:17). We valiantly identify with the pain of our Lord, who endured the cross for us. (See 1 Peter 4:12-13.)

Stake-driving Time

In the Old West, decisions about property lines were finalized with stakes. Once driven into the earth, marking where one's property stopped and another's began, all turmoil and indecision was supposed to cease. The boundary was proclaimed as official.

We need to drive the "courage stake" deeply into the ground—once we have carefully weighed the options.

It comes down to a critical choice which we must all make. Will we be sedentary, "settler" believers—deeply entrenched in our ways? Will we be immobile, traditional to a fault? Or will we be dynamic, "pioneer" Christians? Adventuresome. Ever hopeful. Flexible. Risking. Courageous.

To borrow my wife's term, will we be "pew potatoes" or daring, challenge-seeking believers? We must make this choice.

George Bernard Shaw puts his finger on the crux in this convicting statement:

This is the true joy in life, the being used for a purpose recognized by yourself as a mighty one: the being thoroughly worn out before you are thrown on the scrap heap, and being a force of nature instead of a feverish selfish little clod of ailments and grievances, complaining that the world will not devote itself to making you happy.[3]

Question: Once our stake is driven, will our fears, somehow, evaporate like midday Malibu fog? Not hardly. Problems, difficult people, and heart-thumping trepidation will stalk our paths until we get to heaven.

Nevertheless, in the face of such fears, we can stand tall. As Christians, we have a coping mechanism that nonbelievers lack—a sound, reliable courage that expands as our challenges grow. The hymn is right, "He giveth more grace as the burdens grow greater."

Down deep, almost all of us desire to live a significant life. We see too many around us who, as Henry David Thoreau said, live lives of "quiet desperation." Treading water. Restless. Always anticipating the next stage. Alienated.

We truly hope that our earthly existence can be different. We want to count for something. To have purpose—rather than being just a temporary configuration of atoms.

In no way does that mean we desire to have statues erected in our memories. We just want to be able to say at life's end, "My life was worth living. Things are at least slightly better in the world because I was here."

And there is no way to escape this conclusion: To be able to say this requires taking courageous stands. Through His power. For His purpose. With His people. In spite of opposition.

Now please understand, standing up for eternal values does not preclude other normal activities. We need not grow a beard, move to the desert and meditate 20 hours a day. Perhaps the world has too many religious eccentrics already.

Rather we must, in our world, align our priorities with God's Word and remember to keep Jesus at the center.

---

3. Source of quote unknown.

Paul made tents, Calvin practiced law, Milton wrote poetry, Pascal was a mathematician, Dorothy Sayers wrote mysteries, Mother Hale takes care of Harlem babies. But all took (or take) courageous stands for Jesus.[4]

Focusing on the eternal is bound to lead us more deeply into the world—working for justice for the powerless, bringing healing to the wounded, offering forgiveness to the guilty.

Then, when our life draws to an end, we will rest assured that we have truly made a significant difference. All because of Jesus at work within us. And nothing seems more important.

I came upon the following statement by the eminent philosopher, Soren Kierkegaard, who wrote over 100 years ago. Weigh it carefully. Personalize it. Seriously contemplate its truth.

> One lives only once. If when death comes the life is well spent, that is, spent so that it is related rightly to eternity—then God be praised eternally. If not, then it is irremediable—one only lives once.[5]

Will we give God the permission to begin calling us "courageous"?

Then, with His constant help, will we *be* courageous? Even in the smallest details of our lives?

We must do so. Our fears must never get the best of us. Never!

4. "The Fear of Insignificance," by Daniel Taylor, *Christianity Today,* February 3, 1989, p. 26.
5. Ibid.

STUDY GUIDE

A Word to the Leader

The questions and assignments you will find here are intended for small group study. They are meant to serve as a resource for the group leader.

You'll soon recognize the active nature of these study sections. The more you give, the more you will get. Each section contains material designed to complement and enhance your understanding of the chapters. Feel free to pick and choose from the various suggestions. If something is not appropriate for your group, perhaps you could develop a more pertinent task or question.

A word of warning: some of the study sections require homework assignments—so make sure to look a week ahead at the material.

Your group success depends on participation and preparation. Members must faithfully read the assigned chapters and be ready to interact with others. The leader must always be a step ahead of the group. Read, study, and prepare in advance. With these individual and corporate components in place, you will be enabled to discover the meaning of courage and begin championing the causes that are near and dear to the heart of God.

CHAPTER ONE

1. The author writes that "no word excites and motivates the human spirit more than 'courage.' " Recall an incident in your life where you exhibited courage or saw it demonstrated, in a significant way, by another. Describe the situation to others in your small group. Based on these various stories, try to come to a consensus on a working definition of "courage."

2. We all need daily doses of encouragement—"courage transfusions." Examine the list below and add your own suggestions for encouraging one another. Try to consider "courage transfusions" that would be particularly applicable to those significant others in your world: coworkers, friends, spouse, children.

- Daily Bible reading   • _____
- Thank-you notes   • _____
- Giving compliments   • _____
- Conflict resolution   • _____

3. How would you rate your faithfulness as a Christian on a scale where 1 = wimp and 10 = courageous. Undoubtedly many of us would take the safe way out and pick #5 to both save face and remain humble. However, courage, at the very least, means a commitment to faithfully live life in light of God's commands. Whatever your score, commit yourself again to living courageously for the Lord.

4. Pray together as a group, asking God for a "courage transfusion" as you read and study this book together and seek to practice its implications.

CHAPTER TWO

1. In this chapter's opening illustration the general's *"retreating* to establish better position" exemplified a negative battle strategy. However, in the battle of life a strategy of retreat to regain composure, meditate, and plan for the future can be an effective resource. Rate yourself in the following categories on the life inventory:

- Work
- Personal Life
- Family Life

- Church
- Recreation
- Spiritual growth

1 2 3 4 5 6 7 8 9 10
dissatisfied   satisfied

Where your score should be higher, consider how a dose of courage might help you to improve.

2. Reexamine the subsection—"A Quality that Distinguishes." Courage should not be confused with:
   (a) *impulsive reaction*
   (b) *indifference to fear, pain, or stress*
   (c) *heroic action*

Can you think of examples where you've seen courage misunderstood—where someone's reaction, indifference, or action was wrongly viewed as admirable? Share them with the group.

3. Now that you've read chapter 2, reconsider your discussion and definitions from chapter 1 question #1. Examine them in light of the author's "Courage is:" section of pp. 26-27. Maybe you'll surprise yourself; courage is not simply displayed in overt and explicit ways, but sometimes is evidenced in the simple and implicit. Share an event from the past week where you demonstrated courage.

CHAPTER THREE

1. In this chapter the author describes four forms of courage: (1) fortitude, (2) bravery, (3) valor, and (4) resoluteness. Write down the author's definitions and discuss the different aspects of courage that they encompass.

2. Both Psalms 27 and 31, prayers for deliverance written by David, end with the plea "let your heart take courage" (RSV, KJV). Read these Psalms out loud, discuss the unique problems David was facing in each situation, and focus on how his response of courage enabled him to endure the crises.

3. If you are ambitious, read Stephen Crane's novel, *The Red Badge of Courage*. Although Crane is a naturalist, the soldier in the story emerges as a sort of hero gaining a sense of self-confidence. Discuss the paths taken by the protagonist in his journey of self-revelation.

4. Divide your group into twos. Have each individual pray for the other, focusing particularly on an area where he or she needs to show courage in the coming week.

CHAPTER FOUR

1. Have your group read out loud the Beatitudes (Matt. 5:3-12) of Jesus. Each of the eight beatitudes have both a present and future fulfillment. Discuss how courage plays a role in the nurture and practice of each of these spiritual ideals. Give each member a piece of paper, have them complete their own personal beatitude (below) on courage and share it with the group.

Blessed are the courageous, for _____

_____

2. If Jesus is our "Holy Knight" whose courage (in the form of chivalry) transcends the four types discussed in chapter 3, what was His highest expression of that chivalry? Discuss how we may imitate His holy example of sacrificial living in our everyday lives.

3. Reflecting on examples of Jesus' ministry described in this chapter as well as in the Gospels, have each member share a favorite incident from the life of Christ where He exhibited courage.

4. G.K. Chesterton once wrote, "Courage is almost a contradiction in terms. It means a strong desire to live taking the form of a readiness to die." Discuss this two-sided nature of courage with the group and have members verbalize an area where they need to take a stand for courage in their lives.

CHAPTER FIVE

1. Assign each group member one chapter in John F. Kennedy's *Profiles in Courage*. Have the individuals report back to the group on the contents of the chapters and any new insights into courage they may have gained.

2. God's people have always been populated with "significant insignificants," as evidenced by the lives of Rahab and Ananias. Consider the "significant insignificants" in your local church or fellowship. Share about the jobs/ministries that these people perform and the effect they have on the people around them.

3. Take time to read the stories of the other "significant insignificants" mentioned in the chapter:

- Nathan
- Ruth
- Caleb
- Mordecai

- Joseph
- The generous widow
- Lydia
- Barnabas

Discuss how the actions of these biblical characters evidenced courage in their lives.

4. Many significant parachurch ministries demonstrate courage by ministering in quiet (seemingly insignificant) and nondescript fashion. Select one of these socially-oriented organizations—World Vision, Samaritan's Purse, Compassion International, World Relief—learn about the nature of their ministry and finally, put your pocketbook where your study is: Take a special collection among group members and send the proceeds on to your selected group.

5. "We'll never have ideal conditions that will make Christian courage seem attractive, easy, or convenient. There is always a heavy price to pay—a cost to bear."

Discuss the implications of the author's thesis. Are you willing to commit to courage?

CHAPTER SIX

1. Examine three meanings for courage found in the New Testament and described in chapter 6: (1) courage to speak, (2) courage to do, and (3) courage to be. Discuss the various nuances of the word *courage* that you discover.

2. Invite someone whose job daily calls for courage—such as a fireman or policeman—to address your group on the topic of courage in the workplace. Afterward, ask questions of the guest, reflecting on what you've learned about courage thus far.

3. Recall the biblical principles of courage mentioned in this chapter:
   (1) remembering God's victory in the past
   (2) possessing a stalwart faith
   (3) shaping by trial and persecution
   (4) becoming allergic to the spotlight
   (5) affirming God

Have each member share an incident of courage from their lives that mirrors one of these biblical principles.

4. All of us show courage, at least part of the time. The trick is to learn to endure and persevere in courage. The author offers eight reasons why we frequently shy away from courage. Examine the list and have each member choose one or two of the reasons that most frequently keep them from practicing courage. After sharing the reasons with the group, have each individual write a private prayer to God asking for help in overcoming their fears.

- fear
- authority figure
- "sheep complex"
- "psychic overload"
- crisis motivation
- "shovelers"
- "spectatoritus"
- "heart void"

CHAPTER SEVEN

1. Consider the quotation from James Dobson on page 87. Are things really getting worse in our society? Has there been a loss of integrity? Cite some examples from your own experience.

2. What does the Bible say about integrity? Look up the word *integrity* in a Bible concordance. Review the passages where the word is mentioned and discuss its meaning in context.

3. Study the six stages of moral development as noted by Dr. Lawrence Kohlberg. Using his model, have members reflect on a recent important decision that they made. What developmental stage was reflected in their decision-making process? Discuss the implications of Kohlberg's insights for those seeking to develop courage.

4. Create a role play for the group. Center it on a difficult ethical decision that must be made. Have members "brainstorm" for a possible solution to the dilemma. Work to come to a consensus on the problem. After doing so, look at Kohlberg's preconventional, conventional, and post-conventional development stages. Were any of them reflected in the decision-making process?

5. Read the poem "Myself" out loud. Have group members commit to reading the poem once a day for the following week as an exercise in "courage transfusion."

6. Have members discuss the three things integrity can do for us.

7. Lewis Smedes writes, "No wrong choice . . . can persuade God to love you less. Believe this and you will have new courage to make choices, even when you are not sure they (are) the right ones. . . ." Can members accept Smedes' claim? Have them write down a choice (commitment) in a letter to God, address it to themselves, and give it to the Leader. In three months the Leader will send out the letters.

CHAPTER EIGHT

1a. Consider your relationships at work, home, or school. Do you display compassion in these varied areas of your life?

1 2 3 4 5 6 7 8 9 10

Never   Sometimes   Always

b. To what extent does your score indicate that your "compassion quotient" is deficient?

c. Discuss, as a group, steps you might take to begin exhibiting compassion in your lives. Plan strategies for raising your "compassion quotient."

2. Look up the following Bible verses (NIV). Assign one verse to a group member and have him or her explain its relevancy to the topic of compassion.

- Nehemiah 9:17
- 1 Peter 3:8
- Colossians 3:12

3. Review the story of Ted Stallard whose life was touched by the caring attitude of Miss Thompson. Have participants think about influential people from their pasts—perhaps a teacher, roommate, minister, or friend. Have you ever taken the time to thank that person? Encourage them to contact (by letter or phone) this person from the past and thank them for their inspiration and caring.

CHAPTER NINE

1. A big part of developing courage is learning to take risks. Yet many of us are seemingly paralyzed by "the spoilers"—attitudes that inhibit thinking. Have the group examine the ten "mental locks" (listed on p. 116) and share which of these limit their potential for risk-taking at work, home, and in the church. Consider the roots of these limiting factors. Keep in mind, "Doubt is *never* a bad starting point, if we're not content to remain there."

2. Review the list of biblical heroes who were world-class doubters but who went on to become courageous venturers. While you consider their stories, try to recall other heroes of the faith who had their moments of doubt, but went on to take great risks for God—people such as Peter and Paul. Have members write key characteristics in the lives of these men and women of faith.

3. If we are to learn to be courageous by taking risks, we must learn to dream good dreams. Using the author's paraphrase of Philippians 4:8, have group members plug in the people, ideas, and dreams that they identify with when meditating on this passage: "Whatever is *true*, whatever is *noble*, whatever is *right*, whatever is *pure*, whatever is *lovely*, whatever is *admirable*—we will dream on these things."

4. How can we begin to take risks? Examine the suggestions on page 122. How can members add to that list? Have them look at their responses to question 3. Are they taking any risks with these people, ideas, and dreams that they hold so dear? If not, here is an opportunity to begin.

5. "Where there is no vision, the people perish" (Prov. 29:18, KJV). With this passage in mind, divide the group into pairs and have them commit one-on-one to a risk-taking (dream) activity this next week.

CHAPTER TEN

1. The cost of courage is frequently segregation; the result of taking a stand is often solitude. This was certainly evident in the lives of the various biblical leaders mentioned in this chapter. But what about the twentieth century? Have a group member research the life and death of German pastor and theologian Dietrich Bonhoeffer, who was martyred under the rule of Adolph Hitler during WWII, and report back to the group.

2. Look on the world landscape today. Do you see other examples of men and women taking courageous stands because of their faith? Who are they and what are they doing?

3. Today's courageous Christian must have "sufficient inner resources to stand alone—even to face fierce opposition—in obeying the Lord." Talk about these inner resources and how we can develop them in one another.

4. Examine and discuss the three attitudes for survival we all need in our S.O.S. kits:

- Always remember that ours is a "chosen" loneliness.
- We must accept our loneliness without "excess baggage."
- As our courage is God's gift, so our loneliness is born by His grace.

Have the group share which of these attitudes they have the most difficult time accepting/understanding.

5. Pair off into prayer partners and have members pray for the courage to stand alone when God calls for such a commitment.

CHAPTER ELEVEN

1. Christian courage requires great commitment. It is evidenced by our relationships to (1) a Person, (2) people, and (3) principles. Take time to examine these three areas of your life. If you are truly serious about them then this should be expressed regularly. Answer the following questions with this in mind.

- Do you daily spend a "quiet time" with God?
- Do you faithfully set aside "quality time" to spend with family, coworkers, and friends?
- Do you regularly practice a "quiz time" to examine yourself and the commitments you hold dear?

2. Look at 1 Thessalonians 5:11-18. Turn to the "checklist for encouragers" on page 145. Have the group go through the thirteen examples in the checklist attaching the names of people, where appropriate, whom they can involve in the suggested application. Have members make a list of these people and commit them to prayer in the coming week, asking God for the opportunity to encourage them.

3. The chapter makes a strong case for convictions. Courageous Christians will express their commitment to God by the convictions they hold and practice. The author suggests several of his personal convictions. Go around the group, having participants share their personal convictions and explain why they are important to them. How do individuals stand up for these beliefs?

4. Have the group consider all they've learned in their study so far. How does the call of Christ affect your commitments to courage? If you are unhappy about this area of your life, what must you do to renew your commitments to the Lord and His people?

CHAPTER TWELVE

1. Divide the group in two: have one group discuss blind loyalty and the other one convinced loyalty. Brainstorm for examples from the lives of group members. Have the two groups come together and explain their discoveries.

2. Review the subsection "Fool's Gold." The author mentions job, family, and money as primary loyalty areas. Consider these three along with others mentioned below. What are some kinds of fool's gold that many of us grasp for? Have the group place a check beside areas of temptation and discuss them.

Job ____	Celebrities ____	Home ____
Family ____	Nature ____	Sports ____
Money ____	Hobbies ____	Cars ____
Friends ____	Service clubs ____	Food ____

3. Have the group pair off and share responses to the following questions.

- What does loyalty mean to you?
- What is the price of loyalty?
- How can Christians show loyalty in this generation?

4. "Perhaps it is under conditions of persecution that we achieve our closest intimacy with, and greatest loyalty to, the Saviour." Have them reflect on the author's statement and write down a time in their lives when they felt a special intimacy with the Lord. Then discuss, as a group, what fostered this intimacy. Was it the result of persecution or suffering? Or something else?

5. Pair the members off again and have each group of two pledge an oath of loyalty to one another. This loyalty oath may be expressed in (a) a commitment to regularly pray for the other person, (b) a promise to help another with a task, or (c) a pledge to perform some Christian service together.

A PARTING WORD

1. Read and reflect as a group on the following prayer penned by H. Reinhold Niebuhr. You may be familiar with it already, but what new insight do you bring to understanding it after your study on courage?

"God, grant me the serenity to accept things I cannot change, courage to change things I can, and wisdom to know the difference."

2. The author closes with the challenge of a critical choice we must make. Will we be sedentary "settler" believers? Or will we be courageous "pioneer" Christians? Ask individuals what their decision will be.

3. As a group, have members share the benefits they gleaned from this book and study. Write them on a chalkboard or overhead transparency.

4. Conclude with a time of corporate prayer and encouragement. Use it as an opportunity for "courage transfusion."

SUBJECT INDEX

SCRIPTURE INDEX